water features
for your
garden

water features for your garden

an inspirational guide to planning and planting

Peter McHoy

HERMES HOUSE

This edition is published by Hermes House

© Anness Publishing Limited 2000, 2003

Hermes House is an imprint of
Anness Publishing Limited
Hermes House
88–89 Blackfriars Road

London SE1 8HA tel. 020 7401 2077; fax 020 7633 9499; info@anness.com

IA CIP catalogue record for this book is available from the British Library

Publisher: Joanna Lorenz
Senior Editor: Caroline Davison
Text Editors: Jeremy Smith & Emma Hardy
Production Controller: Wendy Lawson
Designer: Mark Latter
Illustrator: Neil Bulpitt

Previously published as *Rock & Water Gardens*

1 3 5 7 9 10 8 6 4 2

■ **PAGE ONE**
A bamboo water spout
pouring over rocks into
a pool stocked with
floating aquatic plants
provides an exquisite
hint of the beauty of
oriental style.

■ **PAGE TWO**
Nothing evokes an
atmosphere of serenity
quite like water lilies
floating on a pond. In
summer, their delicate
array of colours will
illuminate the garden.

■ **PAGE THREE**
Rock and water are
made for each other.
The cool qualities of
the still pond water
temper the rough-edged
appeal of the rocks
and plants.

■ **ABOVE**
This duckweed should
be removed before it
has a chance to spread.
It is very hardy and
spreads quickly, so
make sure that you
check for it regularly.

■ **OPPOSITE**
For smaller ponds,
miniature water lilies
like *Nymphaea*
'Pygmaea Helvola'
are ideal, and pretty
enough to command
all the attention.

CONTENTS

INTRODUCTION

Few garden features are more thrilling than the sight of water tumbling over rough-hewn rocks or a rocky outcrop smothered with gloriously coloured alpines. For centuries, gardeners have sought to introduce these elements into their designs. Water features, in particular, were an indication of status and wealth, as is typified by the gardens at the Villa d'Este in Tivoli, east of Rome, or at Versailles, near Paris. The French Impressionist, Claude Monet, drew inspiration from his seductive water gardens at Giverny, outside Paris, when creating some of his most famous paintings. Similarly, alpine gardening has many apostles, who delight at the sight of this diverse group of plants that thrive so successfully on mountain ranges throughout the world. Rock and gravel gardens are also a great idea for the weekend gardener who requires a garden that is relatively low on maintenance, yet high on style. In this book you will find a host of ideas for introducing rock and water into gardens of all sizes.

■ ABOVE

Stratiotes aliodes is a floating water plant.

■ OPPOSITE

Rock and water features can grace even
the smallest of gardens.

ROCK GARDENS

A rock garden is a striking garden feature and provides a perfect environment for growing alpines. The rock gardens in this book range from the highly stylized to the less formal in design. You can introduce rock into your garden in a number of ways, such as positioning rough-hewn rocks in a random fashion for an informal effect or using rocks to disguise a lack of height or create an undulating effect. People tend to associate rock gardens with rockeries, but they also encompass gravel gardens, a low-maintenance alternative to the traditional lawn.

Rock plants are among the most fascinating of flowering plants and a useful plant directory at the back of the book will help you choose a variety of plants, from alpines to dwarf conifers.

WATER GARDENS

Introducing a water feature to the garden will captivate old and young alike. There is nothing quite as effective as the sound of running water to soothe and relax you after a busy and stressful day. There are water gardens to suit most tastes, whether you prefer a geometric formal pool or an irregularly shaped informal pond. A section on wildlife ponds shows you how you can greatly enhance the balance of wildlife in your garden by creating a pond that attracts a variety of animals and birds.

If you prefer the sound of running water and do not have room for a full-scale pool, consider installing a water feature such as a wall-mounted fountain, a bubble fountain or a water spout, all of which are suitable for families with small children.

Many plants are suitable for water gardens and the directory at the back of the book gives information on water lilies and other deep-water aquatics, bog plants, marginals, oxygenators and surface floaters.

THE JAPANESE INFLUENCE

In the past, gardens in Japan were largely created as places for meditation. Stone and water were used to represent strong forces in nature, and are still of great symbolic importance in gardening today. If you want to bring a hint of the orient into your garden, opt for water basins, boulder fountains, and sand and gravel gardens.

■ **ABOVE**
Japanese-style features give subtle elegance to a garden. Here, without being brash or showy, a zig-zag bridge in an oriental water garden makes a dramatic statement.

■ **LEFT**
In the heat of summer, an informal pond will refresh a dusty garden. Here, excavated soil has been used to make a raised bed, which is retained with local stone and log edging. A pond like this will provide a haven for a wide variety of wildlife.

■ **OPPOSITE**
Nothing is more captivating than the sight and sound of water tumbling over rough-hewn rocks. A feature such as this takes a degree of skill to create, but it is undoubtedly a centrepiece certain to draw admiring glances.

ROCK GARDENS

Few materials can rival the beauty of natural stone, so why not add a rock feature to your garden? Rock gardens make fascinating features in their own right. They are incredibly versatile, require little maintenance and can add shape and definition to the garden. A rock garden lends a rugged grandeur to an ordinary garden, and can add a sense of height to low-lying land, creating an impression of gradients in a garden bereft of natural undulations.

Rock gardens can be incorporated into gardens of all sizes. They give the small gardener a great deal of scope, for they allow a large number of alpine plants to be grown in a small area. A well-planted rock garden will provide colour in your garden all year round.

There is a variety of ways in which rocks can be used, ranging from simple tessellations to heaped arrangements that create the impression of a scree. Mix stone and gravel together to contrast their textures, or, if you have a reasonably sized lawn, add small rocky outcrops to create eye-catching focal points.

■ ABOVE
A traditional rock garden can be planted with a host of colourful alpines.

■ OPPOSITE
A rock garden can be planted with dwarf conifers as well as alpines and other rock plants to add a touch of rugged wildness to any garden.

INSPIRATIONAL IDEAS

Whether formal or freestyle, minimalist or packed with features, successful rock and gravel gardens need careful planning.

■ BELOW

Courtyard and enclosed gardens can be cosy and private, especially if surrounded by high walls. By keeping the central part open, an impression of space is given, but a strong sense of form and structure is essential to create a "designed" look.

A strong focal point helps to give a garden a sense of design: here a row of lion mask water spouts commands attention. A design like this can look stark without plants, however, so the planting needs to be strong. Potted trees and shrubs have been used to soften the effect while retaining a formal style. Bear in mind that plants in containers require watering every day in dry weather, so it's worth considering an automatic watering system to save on the labour.

■ OPPOSITE TOP
Gravel has been used here to create a
pleasing setting for the plants, as well as
to suppress weed growth. The carefully
placed stones and potted plants complement the loosely planted dimorphothe-
cas. These daisy-like annuals are easy to
grow and bloom prolifically.

Succulents such as echiums and *Agave
americana* 'Variegata' should be placed
in a frostproof place for the winter.

■ RIGHT
This strongly patterned design shows
excellent use of line and form, mass and
void – all elements of good design. It
was created for the Chelsea Flower
Show, London. Granite slabs have been
set into the fine gravel, but for economy
paving slabs could be used instead. Roof
tiles set on edge have been used to create a strong, unusual pattern. The blocks
of low-growing box (*Buxus sempervirens*
'Suffruticosa') can be achieved in a short
space of time if a generous number are
planted close together. This may appear
extravagant, as box is fairly costly, but
very few other plants have to be pur-
chased for this style of garden.

■ LEFT
In contrast to the
rigid formality of
classical gravel
gardens, this dry
garden evokes a
wild landscape.
The seemingly
random placing
of the rocks and
the sloping site
without visible
boundaries are
cleverly planned
to suggest that
this garden is free
from the rigours
of design.
Lavender, santoli-
na and grasses
have been planted
in between the
rocks for colour
and a change of
texture.

Know-how

ON THE ROCKS

Rockwork can be difficult to incorporate into a garden plan, and will be much easier on a sloping site than on a flat one. Don't think only of traditional rock garden banks, however, as rock outcrop beds can be equally pleasing and are much easier to construct in gardens without a natural slope.

PEAKS AND TROUGHS

The most commonly cited drawback to rock gardens is that they are at their best in spring, and by comparison can seem rather dull at other times of the year. Do not allow this to deter you from using rock features. By choosing plants that flower at different seasons, and including evergreens and winter-flowering bulbs for the bleakest months, a rock garden can be packed with interest every month of the year.

Try using annuals to fill in any gaps for the summer, even if they are not strictly alpines, but make sure they don't seed readily and thereby become a nuisance in future seasons.

■ ABOVE LEFT

ROCKERY BORDER An artificial mound in a flat garden does not always work as well as this example, especially if the mound is low and only small pieces of rock are used. This mound is substantial enough to make a positive feature, and it has plenty of evergreens and winter-flowering heathers to make it attractive the year round.
DESIGN TIP *To prevent a rockery from looking stark in winter, be sure to plant sufficient evergreens as well as alpines in this kind of rock garden.*

■ LEFT

SLOPING ROCK GARDEN A gentle slope like this makes an ideal natural-looking rock garden. A rock garden of this size will accommodate a large number of plants and is ideal for anyone who wants to specialize in alpines. A path through the rocks is perfect for viewing these small plants close up.
DESIGN TIP *The natural effect would have been spoilt if the steps had run up through the centre in a straight line. A staggered or meandering path is less obtrusive, and is likely to be less tiring to climb than one that goes straight up by the shortest route.*

■ ABOVE

ROCKY BANKS Rock and water make happy partners, and this weathered limestone is especially attractive. This garden is on the grand scale, but a smaller version could be constructed for a more modestly sized garden.

DESIGN TIP *Follow any natural contours in the ground wherever possible to minimize the amount of earth-moving required.*

■ LEFT

FEATURE ROCKERY This rock feature could be incorporated into most informal designs. It's simply a bed cut into the lawn, and even a small area like this can be densely planted. The rock is tufa, a soft, porous stone into which planting holes can be easily drilled if necessary.

DESIGN TIP *Keep the height of a rock bed in proportion to its size. A small bed should have only a low mound, a large bed can be higher. If you plant densely, as has been done in this rock feature, height is relatively unimportant.*

Know-how

WAYS TO GROW ROCK PLANTS

If your interests lie more with the exquisite beauty of rock garden plants than with the hard landscaping of a rock garden, there are plenty of ways to include alpines in settings far removed from the traditional rockery.

COMBINED WITH WATER

Most rock and water plants prefer a sunny position to thrive, and rocks and water associate well together. It is often possible to introduce a series of cascades linking a small pool at the top with the main pool below. Bury the connecting hose when constructing the rock garden, and use plenty of rocks to make the cascades look as natural as possible. Pleasing rock and water gardens can also be constructed without running water.

GOOD STARTER PLANTS FOR A ROCK GARDEN

There is a huge selection of rock garden plants available. One of the delights of collecting them is the ability to indulge in a wide range of plants that don't take up much space.

- *Acaena microphylla*
- *Antennaria dioica* 'Rosea'
- *Arabis ferdinandi-coburgi* 'Variegata'
- *Armeria maritima*
- *Aster alpinus*
- *Aurinia saxatilis*
- *Campanula carpatica*
- *Campanula cochleariifolia*
- *Dianthus deltoides*
- *Dryas octopetala*
- *Erinus alpinus*

- *Gentiana acaulis*
- *Gentiana septemfida*
- *Gentiana sino-ornata*
- *Geranium subcaulescens* 'Splendens'
- *Gypsophila repens*
- *Helianthemum*
- *Hypericum olympicum*
- *Iberis sempervirens* 'Snowflake'
- *Oxalis adenophylla*
- *Phlox douglasii*

- *Phlox subulata*
- *Pulsatilla vulgaris*
- *Raoulia australis*
- *Saxifraga* (mossy type)
- *Sedum spathulifolium* 'Cape Blanco'
- *Sedum spurium*
- *Sempervivum* (various)
- *Silene schafta*
- *Thymus serpyllum* (various)
- *Veronica prostrata*

ISLAND ROCK BEDS

For reasonably large, informal lawns, creating small rocky outcrops is an ideal way of evoking a wild, rugged landscape . You don't need many rocks in order to create this kind of rock garden, just a few bold ones, carefully positioned so that they look as though they are protruding through the ground. Choose spectacular alpines that will smother the rocks in a wonderful array of colours when summer arrives.

DESIGN TIP *For rocks to look convincing when positioned in a lawn, it is important to slope them into the ground, and for the strata to lie in one direction.*

■ BELOW

RAISED BEDS

Adding a raised bed is a far better way of introducing alpines to a paved area than a number of containers. It will have far greater visual impact, and will not need watering daily during hot spells. You can build the beds with bricks, walling blocks or natural stone.

DESIGN TIP *A series of raised beds is an ideal solution for gardeners who are elderly, infirm or disabled.*

■ ABOVE

ROCK PLANTS IN GRAVEL GARDENS

Rock plants look good in gravel, so include them in a gravel garden or create a small, flat gravel bed just for rock plants. Provide the same soil conditions as for a raised rockery, but on level ground. You can also include a few rocks to create the impression of a scree.

DESIGN TIP *Arrange the plants in their pots before planting, to see how they will look best.*

GRAVEL GARDENS

Gravel and stone gardens are often created using only a few striking plants, allowing the gravel surface and any feature stones to speak for themselves. They are easy to care for, since weed growth is suppressed, especially if partnered by drought-tolerant plants.

■ ABOVE

Gravel and stone gardens are low-maintenance, especially if you plant them with drought-tolerant plants such as lavenders. A few plants go a long way in this kind of garden, and maintenance is limited to trimming back any plants that begin to outgrow their space. This garden was created by Hilliers for the Hampton Court Flower Show, England, and has swirls of different-coloured gravel for extra effect: in your own garden,

subject to regular foot traffic, you may prefer to use only one kind of gravel.

Weeds should not be a problem if the gravel is laid thickly. A plastic sheet laid over the ground first will prevent deep-rooted perennial weeds from becoming a problem. Where necessary, it's possible to plant through the plastic sheet by making slits in the appropriate place with a knife.

■ ABOVE

Sometimes being big and bold within a small area can be extremely effective. Apart from the paving and brick raised bed, this garden contains little more than some large pots and plenty of pebbles and boulders. The use of large plants like *Phormium tenax*, arundinaria (a bamboo), and even a larch (larix) tree, provides plenty of impact. The use of a little colour, like the red nicotianas at the back, works all the better for being set among the greenery.

The choice of a bamboo fence gives the plants sufficient light for good growth while ensuring a good degree of privacy.

■ LEFT

You don't need a large space for a big impact. A small walled area can look stunning if the design is bold enough. Only a few different kinds of plants have been used here, but the varied textures of the garden floor compensate. The straight lines of the decking create an effective contrast with the organic shapes of stone and gravel. Mainly tender plants have been used in this dry garden, which is also a sun-trap. Most of these, like the echeverias in the blue bed in the foreground, will have to be taken in for protection where there are winter frosts, as this is essentially a summer garden.

The use of colour, on the walls and the edges of the beds, combined with the warm tones of the gravel, make this a garden of pleasing textures, colours and shapes even without the plants.

Planning and Planting
In Place of Grass

Sometimes an existing garden can be transformed simply by replacing the lawn. This is especially worth considering if the physical effort of mowing is a problem and you want a low-maintenance garden. In this garden, the lawn was simply replaced by gravel, providing an effective foil to the brilliantly colourful borders.

PLANNING

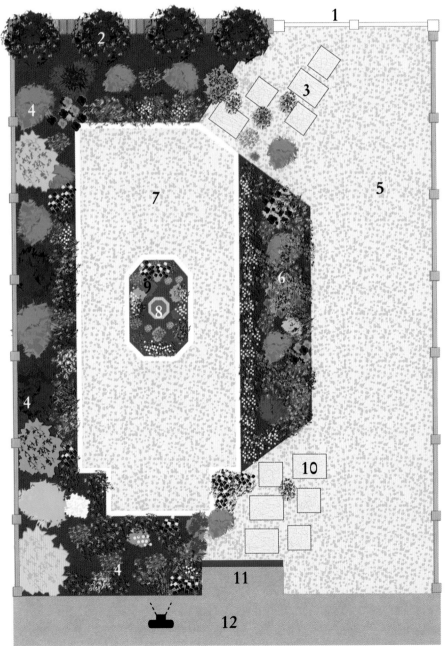

KEY TO PLAN

1 Picket gate
2 Conifers
3 Paving slabs and plants set in gravel
4 Mixed border
5 Gravel drive
6 Roses in mixed border
7 Gravel
8 Birdbath
9 Alpines and low-growing plants
10 Paving slabs set in gravel
11 Front door
12 House

Viewpoint on photograph

Not everyone wants to be involved in a major redesign in order to reduce the amount of time and effort spent on the garden. It may be possible to change a few labour-intensive features, and the lawn is often a priority in this respect. Here it was decided to replace the grass with gravel. Even though weeding and dead-heading would still be demanding at times, it was mowing the lawn that was becoming a chore. The existing beds were left, and the grass lifted and replaced with gravel. To prevent the gravel spreading on to the surrounding beds, an edging was added to keep it in place.

IN REVERSE

If you consider that a garden simply isn't a proper garden without a lawn, but are not too concerned about lots of flowerbeds to look after, you could keep the grass and fill the beds or borders with gravel instead. This will also suppress weeds in the beds. To reduce the amount of grass to mow, it may be worth cutting some new beds into the lawn.

PLANTING

HOW TO MAKE A GRAVEL BED

1 Start by marking out the shape with a rope, hose, or sand sprinkled where the outline should be. Oval-shaped beds are ideal for small gardens.

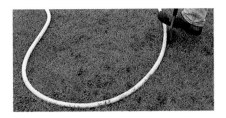

2 Cut the outline of the bed around the hose or rope, using a half-moon edger, or use a spade if you don't have an edging tool.

3 Lift about 10cm (4in) of grass with a spade. Add 7.5cm (3in) of gravel. Leave 2.5cm (1in) gap below lawn level to protect the grass from loose gravel.

4 If you want to plant in the gravel bed, fork in a generous quantity of rotted manure or garden compost, together with a slow-release fertilizer.

5 Allow the compost to settle before adding the gravel. Spread 5–8cm (2–3in) of gravel evenly over the firmed surface, and level it with a rake.

6 Gravel is best planted sparsely with a good space in between plants. Try adding a few stones or pebbles to enhance the effect.

Planning and Planting

CURVES AND LINES

Corner sites can present special problems, but this gravel design has unusually managed to marry straight lines and curves in a successful and distinctive way. It sometimes pays to be bold and imaginative when the site is a difficult one.

PLANNING

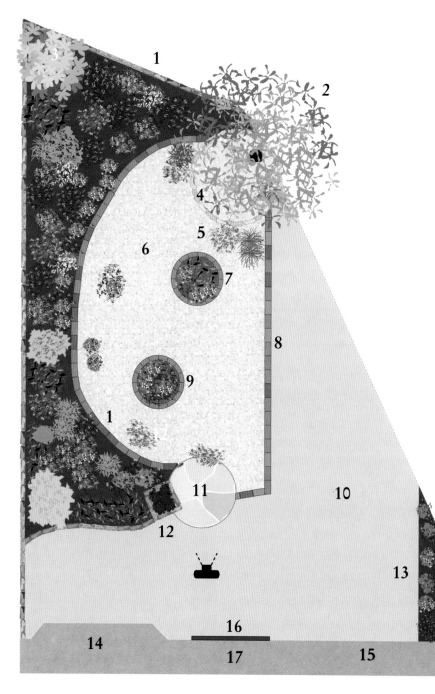

Here, an attractively edged gravel area has been used to transform an awkward corner site bordered by the unyielding line of a driveway.

Maximum use has been made of the existing birch tree in this plan, as it takes the eye from the bleakness of the drive. Creating a circular bed around it emphasizes it as a focal point, and to give the garden a sense of unity, the circular theme has been repeated with a couple of round raised beds and an interesting circular stone feature, linking the drive and gravel area.

USING GRAVEL
Gravel is best laid over a weed-suppressing base, but it's still possible to plant through both materials if necessary.

PLANTING

HOW TO MAKE A WEED-FREE GRAVEL BED

1 Dig the area to hold 5cm (2in) of gravel. Level the ground, then lay heavy-duty black plastic or a mulching sheet over the area. Overlap strips by about 5cm (2in).

2 Tip gravel on to the sheet, then rake it level. To plant through the gravel, draw back an area of gravel from where you plan to plant and make a slit in the plastic.

3 Plant normally through the slit, enriching the soil beneath if necessary with fertilizer or garden compost.

4 Firm in the plant with your hand and water thoroughly, then smooth the plastic back and re-cover the area with gravel.

Planning and Planting

SECLUSION WITH STYLE

The gravel and stones in this stylish garden complement beautifully the handsome wooden patio and raised beds.

KEY TO PLAN

1 Garden wall
2 Timber decking
3 Shrubs and ground cover
4 Raised bed
5 Bamboos
6 Plants in gravel
7 Raised timber patio
8 Pots on stand
9 Stepping stones
10 Rock feature
11 *Festuca glauca*
12 Conservatory
13 Gravel
14 House

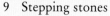 Viewpoint on photograph

PLANNING

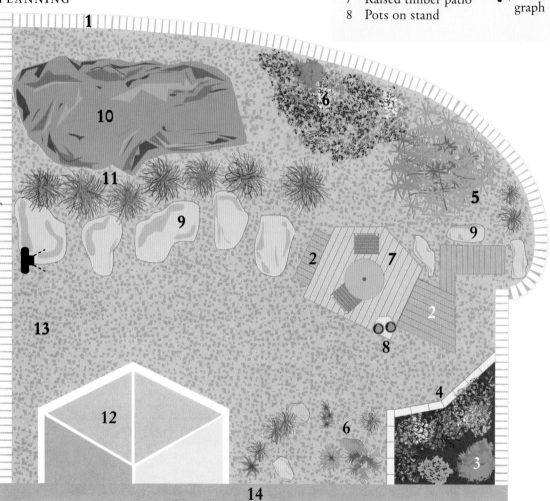

Here, a tall wall provides seclusion and privacy, creating an oasis in which a striking dry garden has been created. The white-painted finish helps to reflect light and provides the perfect backdrop to the dramatic planting.

The wooden patio and raised beds give this garden a stylish air, and the colour of the timber (lumber) is offset beautifully by the pale gravel. The exotic bamboos and the spiny *Festuca glauca* – which look very natural in their stony beds – are the perfect finish.

INEXPENSIVE GROUND COVER

The raised bed in this garden has been planted with shrubs and ground cover. Ground-cover plants share one of the virtues of gravel: they suppress weeds at the same time as covering the ground. If you want the effect of a carpet of foliage, you will need a large number of plants. Keep the cost down by buying a few large plants and taking plenty of cuttings or dividing them if appropriate. Pachysandra is an example of an excellent ground cover that's easy to divide, even if the plant is still young.

HOW TO PLANT GROUND COVER

1 Ground-cover plants that spread by underground runners or have a crown of fibrous roots can be divided easily into three to four small pieces. Water the plant about half an hour before you start.

2 Gently knock the plant out of its pot. If it doesn't pull out easily, just tap the edge of the pot on a hard surface. It should then be possible to pull the plant without damaging the roots.

3 Carefully pull the root-ball apart, keeping as much soil on the roots as possible. Plants with a crown of fibrous roots can be prised apart into pieces using a couple of small hand forks.

4 If the crown is too tough to pull or prise apart with a fork, try cutting through it with a knife. If this is done carefully using a sharp knife, the plant should not be damaged too much.

PLANTING

5 It has been possible to divide this plant into eight smaller ones, but the number you will be able to achieve depends on the size of the original plant.

6 Replant immediately into the gravel or soil, if you don't mind starting with small plants. Otherwise pot up the pieces and grow them on for a year before planting out into the garden. Keep new plants well-watered until they are established.

Planning and Planting
FRAMING A FOCAL POINT

A dry garden like this benefits from a water feature such as a bubble fountain, which emphasizes the arid conditions all around and seems even more refreshing for that. Eye-catching structural features, like the moon gate and the ornament it frames, and the stone-surrounded fountain, render the lack of colourful plants unimportant. They give the garden an impact that will be retained throughout the seasons.

PLANNING

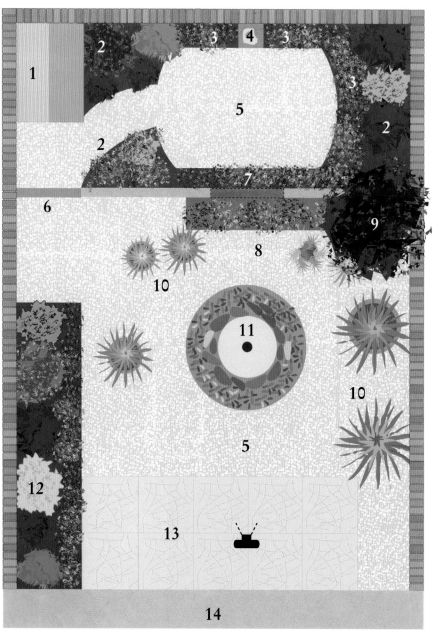

Dividing the garden into smaller sections is a good way to add interest and encourage a sense of exploration. In this garden plan, the construction of a wall with a marvellous moon gate, a circular hole built into the wall, not only provides an outstanding focal point but encourages the viewer to explore the remaining garden beyond the wall. The ornament positioned against the back wall ensures the eye is taken not only to the moon gate but beyond it, and the fountain in the foreground echoes and balances it. The yuccas and phormiums positioned in pots to the right and left help to frame the window in the wall and require less watering than most container-grown plants.

PLANTING

This highly imaginative garden has many unusual features, each of which is special in its own right, and which together interconnect to form a most striking whole. The eye is led down the garden from the stone-surrounded fountain in the foreground, through the moon gate in the wall and finally to the imposing lion's head, and the careful placing of the outsize potted plants helps to direct the eye towards these features.

Gravel has been used here as the perfect foil to the spiky, variegated plants in their giant pots. It is also the ideal surround for the millstone fountain. The gradual change from gravel to pebbles and finally to large stones surrounding the millstone makes the fountain appear to grow out of the ground, as if it were a natural feature and not an artifical construction. This use of a water feature in an otherwise dry garden is highly effective: the soft jet of gently bubbling water provides a pleasing contrast with the arid surrounding of the gravel and the solid structure of the walls.

The division of this garden into two sections gives scope for separate planting schemes. The more formal planting of the first section of this garden, with its one long bed, some low-growing shrubs and the yuccas and phormiums, contrasts with the more relaxed planting in the "room" beyond the wall, where larger shrubs can be seen peeping through the window and where ground cover surrounds another area of gravel. The use throughout this garden of shrubs, ground-cover plants and drought-loving potted plants, in combination with the gravel, makes this an extremely easy garden to look after, since it requires very little maintenance.

Planning and Planting
CHANGING LEVELS

Rock gardens are sometimes used as a design solution for a steep slope, where rock outcrops can look very convincing. If the slope is more gentle and the setting inappropriate for a large conventional rock garden, it may be possible to make the most of a raised rock bed. This one forms a natural break between a level upper lawn and a larger sloping lawn that leads to the rest of the garden.

PLANNING

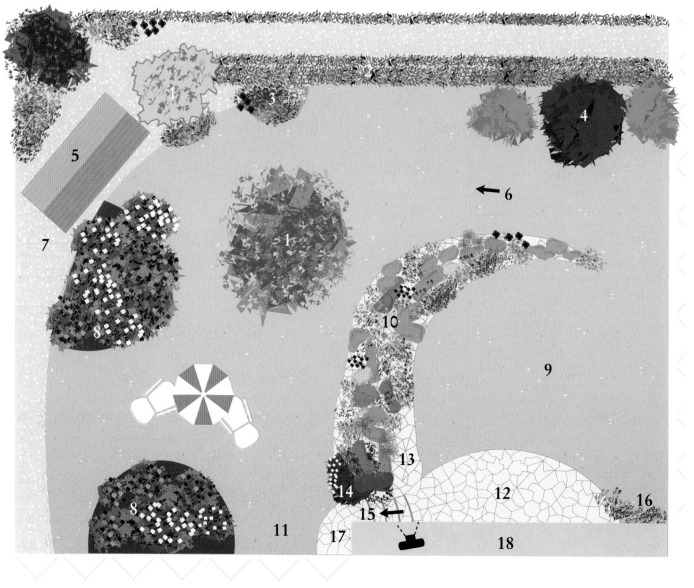

SLOPING GARDENS

Even gently sloping gardens pose the problem of how to integrate the various levels. Steep gardens are often terraced, although this is a labour-intensive and often expensive option. Where the height difference is small enough to make mowing a safe and practical routine, a gently sloping lawn is a sensible option. Here, a flat area of patio and lawn has been created at the front of the house, with the lawn falling away beyond the rock bed.

Rock beds make pleasing features, but they look best where they have a purpose. Here, the rock bed acts as a divider, with the ground falling away more on one side than the other.

MAKING A ROCK GARDEN

A raised rock bed like this one can be made on a level site if necessary, or you could build one at the back of a pond using the excavated soil for the basic mound. In either case, good fertile soil should be used for the planting areas. Locally quarried rocks are usually cheaper and blend in with the area.

PLANTING

HOW TO MAKE A ROCK GARDEN

1 Build up soil to form a raised area of appropriate size. Always ensure there is a space between the soil and any fence or wall, and be careful not to bridge any damp-proof course in nearby brickwork.

2 Mix together equal parts of soil, coarse grit and peat and spread evenly over the mound. Lay the first rocks at the base, trying to keep the strata running in the same direction.

3 Position the next row of rocks. Use rollers and levers to move them. Ensure that the sides all slope inwards, and make the top reasonably flat rather than building it into a pinnacle.

4 Position the plants. As each layer is built up, add more of the soil mixture, and consolidate it around the rocks. Finish by covering the exposed soil with a thin layer of horticultural grit, to improve the appearance.

Planning and Planting
NATURAL SLOPE

Gardens with a gentle slope offer an ideal opportunity for constructing a natural-looking rock and water feature, with perhaps a stream and a small cascade. For ease of construction, these features may have to follow the natural contours of the site, and this may influence your design.

KEY TO PLAN

1	Garden bench	10	Dwarf conifer
2	Lawn	11	Patio
3	Rock garden	12	Plants in containers
4	Slope and step	13	House
5	Pond		
6	Cascade	↑	Direction of steps down
7	Stream		
8	Mixed border		Viewpoint on photograph
9	Header pool		

A naturally sloping garden is ideal for a rock and water feature, but your design will be determined largely by the slope and profile of the ground. Where practical, choose a rock type found in your locality: it will look more natural, and it will almost certainly be cheaper than rock that has been transported over long distances.

Planting plans are difficult to devise for a rocky slope, so concentrate on a few key plants, such as dwarf conifers and dwarf evergreen shrubs. The smaller rock plants are usually best planted intuitively, choosing subjects that fit both the space available and the setting.

A meandering path is always more interesting than a straight one, and a combination of sloping path and a few steps changes the pace and makes the slope easier to cope with.

Seating also requires careful thought. It's worth providing a refuge large enough to take a seat partway down to help those who find slopes difficult. Choosing a position that has an attractive view of the garden, or of the scene beyond, will encourage more use of the seat.

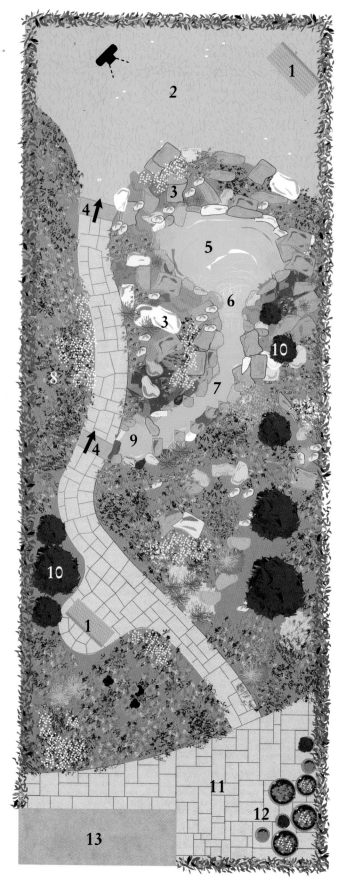

PLANTING

■ RIGHT
MAKING A ROCK STREAM
A stream can be constructed from a series of separate long, narrow ponds, with the liners overlapped and sealed where the levels change.

Use a good-quality liner over a proper liner underlay, and place small concrete slabs at each side of the level changes on which to bed suitable rocks. Fold over a piece of spare liner to form an extra cushion under the concrete pad.

The stream is made watertight at the cascades by lapping the liner from the higher pond over that from the lower (see illustration). This should prevent water escaping, but as an additional precaution seal the overlaps with special tape or adhesive. Consult your aquatic supplier regarding materials, as it depends on the type of liner used.

Bed the rocks firmly on each side of the cascade on mortar to ensure they are stable. You may, however, first want to have a test run, then drain the water to make any adjustments. An aquatic specialist should be able to advise on a suitable pump – it will need to be powerful to maintain a fast flow over a wide lip. A header pool is used at the top, fed by a return hose from the pump.

CROSS-SECTION OF A ROCK STREAM

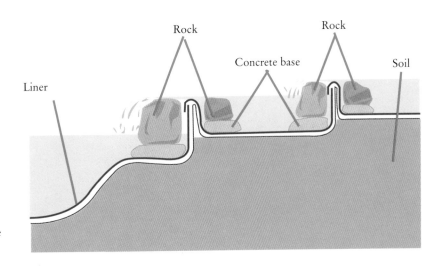

Rock

Rock

Concrete base

Soil

Liner

WATER GARDENS

There are few gardens that would not benefit from the inclusion of a water feature. Water has an almost magical attraction, holding a fascination for both adults and children. The introduction of a pool into a garden has a calming effect, its natural serenity aiding contemplation and relaxation. A formal pond with a distinct, geometric shape is the perfect complement to a highly stylized garden, while for a more natural appearance, an informal pool with a more irregular shape will reflect the beauty of a less rigidly structured garden. A pond will also entice all kinds of wildlife into your garden, making even the most urban of homes seem like a rural enclave. Few sights and sounds are as thrilling as moving water, so use water imaginatively and make the most of the natural contours of your garden to achieve incredible results. From a dramatic baroque-style fountain and cascading water stairs to a gently rippling rill or babbling brook, the options are endless.

■ ABOVE
Iris laevigata prefers moist conditions or shallow water.

■ LEFT
This large pond has been planted with a host of water lilies – here
Nymphaea 'Attraction' which flowers in early summer.

INSPIRATIONAL IDEAS

Ponds and "streams" can form the centre-piece of your design. These will attract an amazing diversity of wildlife, and of course can be stocked with fish – which will become very tame if fed regularly during summer months.

■ ABOVE
A raised formal rectangular pond can be constructed from bricks or building blocks, rendered inside and out. It can be waterproofed using special resins or bitumen products obtainable from a pond supplier. The render on the outside can be painted a light colour to create a more attractive feature. Raised ponds are particularly useful for anyone who is disabled or infirm, or who finds bending difficult, as they bring the underwater wonders that much closer to eye level.

■ ABOVE

Imagine this scene as an ordinary lawn with just the borders at each side: pleasant but a trifle boring and without a strong sense of design. A simple pond in isolation would have been equally unappealing because there would be no sense of setting or height, and in winter it could look bleak and uninviting. Setting the pond in a larger circular area, however, with crescents of borders, paths and pebble areas, has given this section of the garden a sense of cohesion and design. The pebbles cleverly merge border and pond, and the sloping beach that drops away into the pond provides easy access for wildlife.

■ LEFT

In this water feature, the water flows directly into a submerged reservoir beneath a strong grille that supports the stone and boulders, making it safe for even small children. Occasionally, genuine millstones are used for this kind of feature, but these are extremely heavy to handle and support, as well as being expensive and difficult to obtain. Fortunately, convincing glass-fibre imitations that look just as good, and which are much easier to handle and install, are available. You can buy them as part of a kit that includes the reservoir, and all you have to provide are the boulders or pebbles.

Although these kinds of feature can be set among plants, they tend to look most effective in a courtyard or dry-looking area as shown here.

Know-how

WATER AND WILDLIFE

Adding water features such as ponds or waterfalls helps to create an aesthetically pleasing garden for as that wildlife also finds attractive. Often these demands are in conflict, but with a little imagination it's possible to combine both aims.

Water is a magnet for wildlife of all kinds, not just amphibians and aquatics. For those with children, there are some simple, safe water features that will provide an opportunity for wildlife to visit to drink and bathe. Even a birdbath is better than no water at all.

■ BELOW
PONDS A pond like this makes an attractive feature in its own right, and can form the centrepiece around which the garden is designed, but it will also bring the bonus of wildlife that otherwise would not visit the area.
DESIGN TIP *An informally shaped pond with easy access from the edges is more likely to attract wildlife than a formal one which is difficult to reach.*

■ ABOVE

STREAMS Anyone lucky enough to have a natural stream running through their garden is fortunate indeed, and will almost certainly have plenty of visiting wildlife. For those less fortunate, it's possible to create a very convincing man-made stream like this one.

DESIGN TIP *To make an artificial stream look truly convincing, plant densely up to the water's edge, using plenty of native plants.*

■ ABOVE

SMALL WATER FEATURES Everyone has space for a simple wildlife water feature like this. It's only an old dustbin (trash-can) lid filled with pebbles and placed over a reservoir with a small pump that recirculates the water through the frog's mouth. Although it won't support amphibians or insect life, it will make a water hole for birds and many mammals.

DESIGN TIP *Use this kind of feature to bring movement and life to an otherwise dull part of the garden, perhaps in a very shady spot where few plants thrive.*

■ RIGHT

BANKS Don't be afraid to use native plants and garden plants together if it helps to create the right illusion. This pond bank has a very natural appearance despite being planted with many cultivated plants.

DESIGN TIP *The larger the expanse of water, the more important it is to plant the banks imaginatively unless it is intended to create a void or texture within a formal setting.*

Know-how

NATURAL INFORMALITY

Informal ponds are usually easier to construct than formal ones and are preferred by wildlife because access to the water is usually easier and the surrounding planting provides useful shelter. Informal ponds also provide an excuse to introduce a bog garden.

■ LEFT

NATURAL POND
This garden is completely informal, yet it has a strong sense of design and structure, which the bridge and trellis help to emphasize. The irregular informal shape and rocks give the illusion of a natural pond, and the lush planting helps to mask neighbouring gardens.
DESIGN TIP *An informal pond can be used to encourage a sense of exploration and may make your garden seem larger than it really is. Having access around all sides, or a bridge linking paths, will appear intriguing.*

■ RIGHT

PEBBLES This kind of natural-looking water course can be created easily with a liner, the edge of which can be well hidden by beach pebbles. With this kind of covering, a drop in water level though evaporation will not be noticeable as there is no obvious water line. It must flow into a deep area at the end, however, so that the submerged pump remains covered.
DESIGN TIP *Don't think only in terms of fish ponds when introducing water. Features like this one can be even more effective if you want to create the illusion of a wild or natural garden. They will still attract lots of wildlife which will come to the garden to drink and bathe.*

CLEAR WATER

Even the most well-designed pond will be unattractive if the water is green. Most ponds turn green for a few days or weeks each year, usually in spring and early summer when the water is warming up, but the aquatic plants are not sufficiently grown to reduce the amount of sunlight reaching the water. A pond that remains green for long periods requires treatment.

Green water is caused by millions of free-floating algae, which feed on nutrients in the water, multiplying rapidly in warm, sunlit water. Avoid adding nutrient-rich soil to the pond, and do not use ordinary fertilizer on pond plants.

There are chemical controls of various kinds, but they vary in effectiveness, their effect can be short-lived, and the dead algae can cause problems with falling oxygen levels as they decay (which may kill fish). The most satisfactory way
to deal with green water is to install a UV (ultra-violet) clarifier. This will require a power supply for the special lamp and a pump to circulate the water. Provided you choose a unit powerful enough for the capacity of your pond (consult your supplier), the water should begin to clear within days.

■ RIGHT

CLOSE TO THE HOUSE This pond has been taken up to the conservatory, then a deck has been built out over the water. Pondlife, especially the fish, can be enjoyed from the deck on a sunny day and from the conservatory when the weather is less inviting.
DESIGN TIP *Use plants to create privacy and a sense of seclusion. Here the dense planting masks a busy road.*

■ ABOVE

STREAM-FED POND Regular clearing and planting with a range of water lilies and other plants has transformed this natural stream-fed pond into a wonderful garden feature. The banks have been planted for year-round interest, and ornaments provide useful focal points in winter when most of the vegetation has died down.
DESIGN TIP *Don't forget to incorporate a few garden seats, even in an informal garden. You will get more out of your garden if there's somewhere to sit and relax. Here, the addition of a couple of colourful cushions has transformed an ordinary garden bench into a comfortable focal point from which to view your garden.*

Know-how

FORMAL PERFECTION

Water features can easily be added to an existing garden, but they will look more integrated if you plan for them early on in the design process. Formal ponds are suitable for gardens with a strong sense of design, and although they offer less scope than informal ponds for poolside planting, they are perfect for aquatic plants and surrounding pot plants.

If you want fish and flowers in your pond, choose an open site that will receive sun for at least half the day if possible, and is away from overhanging deciduous trees unless you are prepared to net the pond and clear the leaves from the water to prevent pollution. The majority of rock plants also require a sunny position.

Formal ponds, with their regular outlines and geometric shapes, look best in gardens designed to a rigid grid where the same lines are carried through to other parts of the garden. They offer less scope for pondside planting and associated bog areas than informal ponds do, but provide plenty of scope for aquatic plants and fish.

■ **BELOW**
BREAKING UP PAVING Although this pond is relatively small, it makes an impact because it forms a focal point in a strongly geometric design. Water can be a vital element in counteracting the potential harshness of a large amount of paving. The wall mask ensures the area will remain attractive even when the pond plants have died back.
DESIGN TIP *To avoid an expanse of paving appearing monotonous, use materials of a contrasting colour to pick out a design or to emphasize a change of level. Here, bricks and terracotta tiles have been used to provide contrast and to add a touch of colour to a large area of paving.*

■ **LEFT**
LONG AND FORMAL Formality is the essence of this style of garden, and water is the central feature around which the garden has been designed. It is essentially a garden for a warm climate, or at least where the illusion of a warm-climate garden is required, but a variation on this style of gardening could make a stunning town garden.
DESIGN TIP *Where water is a major feature, always consider how the garden will look in winter. Pumps will have to be turned off in very cold climates, and a pond's frozen surface can look bleak. To compensate, include plenty of evergreens and make lavish use of decorative pots and ornaments around the water feature.*

■ BELOW
UNUSUAL SHAPES Formal ponds are practical for even a small front garden, and the strong design and impressive planting in this one ensure it will be pleasing all the year round. The introduction of a stepping platform to connect the two ponds ensures they link the garden rather than divide it.

DESIGN TIP *If the visual aspects of gravel appeal but you are worried about the loose stones being kicked around on a path that is used frequently, consider bonded gravel, which has been used on these paths. The small stones are bonded to a resin instead of being laid loose. The effect is equally as attractive as loose gravel.*

■ ABOVE
CASCADES A garden created on a gentle slope provides scope for cascades and tumbling water, and in this garden the formal water chute and rectangular pond reflect the overall design, with its straight lines and right angles.

DESIGN TIP *Allow the overall design of the garden to dictate the style of pond you create. In this garden, with its dominant straight lines, an informal wildlife pond with meandering outline and shallow beaches around the edge would have looked incongruous.*

RECTANGULAR PONDS
....

Rectangular ponds can be constructed with a liner, but this involves pleating it at the corners, which can look unattractive unless masked by careful planting. It is possible to have box-welded liners made by specialist suppliers, otherwise render a concrete or building-block pond and waterproof it with a resin or bitumen-based product manufactured for the purpose.

Know-how

MOVING WATER

Still water brings calm and tranquillity to a garden, but sometimes a sense of vibrancy and life is needed. A tumbling "stream" introduces an authentic feeling of the wild to a garden, but sound and movement can be created with equal effect by a tinkling fountain, a tumbling cascade or a simple water spout fixed to a wall. Whichever you choose, moving water is almost certain to become one of the garden's most exciting focal points.

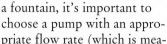

■ RIGHT
WATER STAIRS
Although an ambitious project,
a flight of water stairs can be attention-grabbing as well as musical. Building them on a curve makes the most of the limited space available, and in this case the feature makes a splendid centrepiece for the garden.
DESIGN TIP
Don't be put off by an ambitious project simply because you lack construction skills. Hire a contractor to do the building to your own specific designs.

THINK ABOUT FLOW
....
Whether installing a cascade or a fountain, it's important to choose a pump with an appropriate flow rate (which is measured in gallons or litres an hour). This is a complex area as it also depends on whether the same pump has to share the operation of a biological filter, or perhaps another cascade or fountain. Go to a reputable water garden specialist for advice. Some will even allow you to exchange the pump if it does not do the job.

Large flows will require a high-voltage pump, but most small fountains operate satisfactorily from a low-voltage pump.

■ LEFT
SMALL FOUNTAIN Without moving water, even well-designed small patio ponds may lack impact. A fountain will add to the formal atmosphere, and in a small garden the sound will not be as potentially overpowering as that from a cascade.
DESIGN TIP *Corners can be difficult areas to fill creatively, but a corner pond with an attractive fountain will make excellent use of otherwise wasted space.*

■ OPPOSITE
MOORLAND STREAM It takes years of experience and a lot of effort to construct a moorland stream to this standard, including a knowledge of the natural landscape and the mechanics and flow rates of pumps, but a more modest version is within the scope of an enthusiastic amateur.
DESIGN TIP *Unless your garden is on a natural slope, keep the fall from top to bottom of the "stream" relatively modest. This will avoid too much earth-moving and reduce the need to manhandle heavy rocks, yet the effect can be just as stunning as cascades with large falls.*

■ RIGHT
WALL FOUNTAIN A wall fountain can transform any backyard or courtyard wall. A trickling spout of water will add to the visual and auditory pleasures of the garden. This one is particularly ornate, but in an area where there may not be much else to arrest the attention, being bold can bring rich rewards.
DESIGN TIP *Bear in mind that the higher the position of the water spout above the receptacle, the louder the sound will be. In a confined area, a strong flow from a height could become irritating for you or your neighbours. Fortunately, most pumps have a flow adjuster.*

Planning and Planting

IN A NATURAL SETTING

This garden successfully marries a formal garden with the informality of a woodland area. A small pool forms an integral part of the geometric design, and should attract any wildlife visiting the neighbouring trees and rough grass.

This garden has a strong sense of design in the area immediately in front of the house, combining differently shaped rectangles and squares. It includes a small pool, with a shallow sloping beach at one

PLANNING

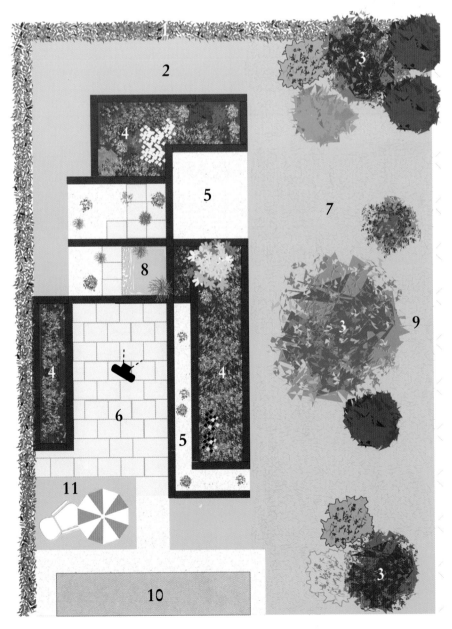

end for a bathing area for birds. The pool is directly in front of the seating area so that the owners can watch any visiting wildlife. The strong sense of line and the different surface textures used in the formal garden ensure it always looks interesting, with many shade-tolerant foliage plants playing an important role.

A woodland area containing rough grass and trees runs along one side, with the hope of attracting wildlife to the garden. Because it is less stimulating to look at than the paved and planted areas, it was placed to the side of the garden.

PRE-FORMED PONDS
Your design may require a small informally shaped pool, and a pre-formed pond is a quick and easy solution. If the ponds are displayed on their sides, lay them on the ground before buying as they may look smaller from a normal viewing position.

PLANTING

HOW TO INSTALL A PRE-FORMED POND

1 Transfer your shape to the ground by inserting canes around the edge of the pond. Run a hosepipe (garden hose) or rope around the outside of the canes.

2 Remove the pond and canes and excavate the hole to approximately the required depth, following the profile of the shelves as accurately as possible.

3 Place a straight-edged piece of wood across the rim of the hole to check that it is level. Measure down to confirm that you have dug to the required depth.

4 Put the pond in the hole, then add or remove soil to ensure a snug and level fit. Remove any large stones. Check with a spirit level that the pond is level.

5 *(right)* Remove the pond, then line the excavation with damp sand if the soil is stony. With the pond in position, and levels checked again, backfill with sand or fine soil, being careful not to push the pond out of level.

6 *(right)* Fill with fresh water from a hose pipe and backfill further if necessary as the water rises, checking the levels frequently as backfilling often lifts the pond slightly. The pond is now ready to fill with plants and wildlife.

A SANCTUARY GARDEN

This garden, with its pleasing combination of water, flowers and woodland, is a sanctuary for wildlife, and also a place where the gardener can retreat from the pressures of everyday life. Three elements that are strongly attractive to wildlife are woodland shelter, water and flowers rich in nectar and pollen. This garden is designed to provide all three.

PLANNING

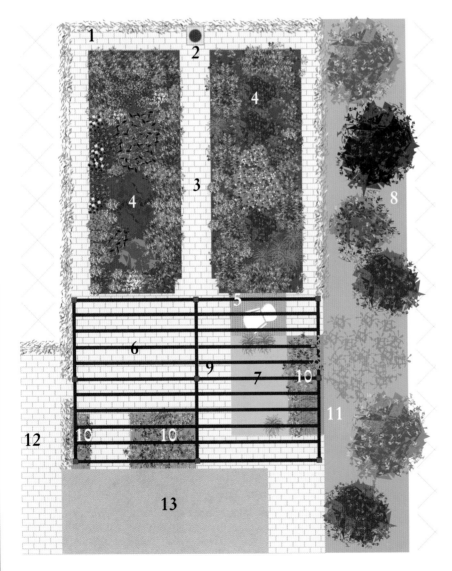

KEY TO PLAN

1 Yew Hedge
2 Animal ornament on plinth
3 Path of concrete pavers
4 Mixed island border containing shrubs, border plants and annuals to attract butterflies and other insects
5 Timber decking
6 Patio of concrete pavers
7 Pond
8 Adjoining woodland
9 Pergola
10 Shrubs
11 Boundary left open to adjoining woodland
12 Parking area
13 House

✕ Garden continues

You might be tempted to plant lots of wild flowers in order to create a wild-looking garden, but, in a garden such as this, with its fairly rigid structure, it's best to concentrate on cultivated ornamentals that are rich in nectar or pollen. These can then be enjoyed by insects.

Although many annuals, and some outstanding herbaceous perennials, are ideal, shrubs are essential to prevent the beds looking flat and uninteresting in winter. If you include berried shrubs such as cotoneasters, these will provide food for birds in autumn and winter.

FLEXIBLE LINERS

A flexible pond liner gives you control over the design of your pond and is suitable for an informal pond since it can be cut and folded to fit any shape of hole. To calculate the size of a liner, measure the maximum length and width of the pool. Then add on twice the depth to each measurement, plus an additional 15cm (6in) all round to allow for an overlap around the edge. The deepest point of the pool should be a minimum of 45cm (18in).

USING A FLEXIBLE LINER

1 Mark out the shape of the pond with a length of garden hose or rope, then remove any turf and start to excavate the pond.

2 Make a shelf all around the pond (or at one end only) for the marginal plants.

3 Check the level as you work. Correct any discrepancies by mounding up the soil on one side and remove any sharp stones. Line with builder's sand.

4 Spread the underlay recommended by the manufacturer of the liner into the hole. You could also use an old piece of carpet or some wet newspaper.

5 Ease the liner into the hole. Cover the base with a layer of topsoil about 7.5cm (3in) deep, then fill the pond with water.

6 Once the pond is full, trim back any excess liner to leave an overlap of about 15cm (6in) around the edge.

7 For a neat finish, lay paving around the edge of the pond. In order to disguise the liner, overlap the water's edge by about 2.5cm (1in).

8 The resulting pond is fairly informal. To make the effect still more informal, arrange a selection of container plants to soften the edges.

Planning and Planting

MODERN IMAGE

Instead of thinking of ponds and cascades when designing with water in mind, try visualizing water as a texture, rather like an area of paving or gravel. This garden shows how smart water can look in a modern setting. Don't be afraid to use water imaginatively: although the amount used in this garden is small, it's one of the most interesting and creative features in an already fascinating and exciting garden.

KEY TO PLAN

1 Bed with dwarf shrubs and border plants
2 Pergola with climbers over
3 Paving
4 Water
5 Raised bed under pergola
6 Island bed
7 Lawn
8 Small trees
9 Fern bed
10 Moisture-loving plants in pebbled planting bed
11 Steps
12 Grass strip
13 Ornamental stone feature
14 House

↑ Direction of steps down

Viewpoint on photograph

PLANNING

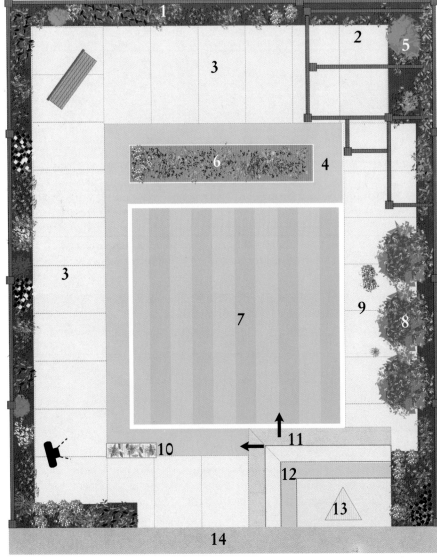

As this garden makes the most of shapes and textures, it is likely to appeal to someone who loves to explore design ideas rather than to a plant enthusiast. Apart from the lawn, which requires regular cutting, it's also very low-maintenance. The water-framed lawn is perhaps the main focal point, so it's essential that the grass is kept short and looking lush, and care must be taken not to allow grass clippings to fall into the watery surround.

Ordinary paving slabs could have been used for economy, but the choice of a natural stone such as slate gives it a more sophisticated appearance and a stronger sense of design. Where paving is a dominant feature in a garden, it is worth spending time and money to select the most suitable material.

Where natural stone forms an important part of the design, it is worth visiting a few stone merchants or quarries to discuss your requirements in detail. They may be able to advise and perhaps assist with the selection and cutting of the stone.

PLANTING

■ RIGHT
PERGOLA POSSIBILITIES Although rustic poles are often used for rose pergolas, in design terms a sawn timber (lumber) pergola is a better choice. It will also be able to support heavy climbers such as wisterias. Use preservative-treated wood (but avoid using creosote if planting soon after erection), and treat cut surfaces before assembling. Fix the uprights securely, setting them in concrete or securing them in post spikes, always using a spirit level to check verticals.

Assemble the overhead sections "dry" on the ground to make sure the joints all fit well, but don't nail them yet. Halving joints are suitable for the overhead beams, but the lower halves will have to be nailed to the uprights before the top halves are assembled.

The halving joints are best screwed together, but drill starter holes while the assembly is on the ground, as it will be difficult to drill at a height.

If the pergola is long, overhead beams will have to be joined, which should be done over a post. Use galvanized nails or zinc-plated screws.

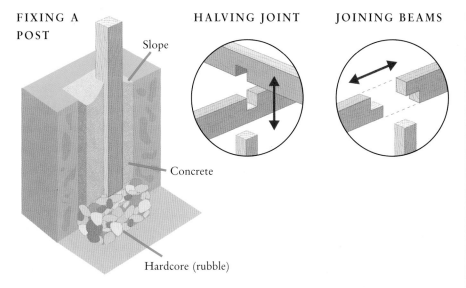

FIXING A POST

Slope

Concrete

Hardcore (rubble)

HALVING JOINT

JOINING BEAMS

Planning and Planting

FOCUS ON CIRCLES

Circular themes are almost always distinctive, and they make striking gardens even with minimal planting. This kind of garden depends very much on structure for impact, and the focal point here is a fantastic water feature that uses both sight and sound to command attention.

PLANNING

1 Specimen tree
2 Ground-cover plants
3 Raised bed
4 Brick paving
5 Raised pool
6 Cascade
7 Dwarf shrubs
8 Specimen shrub
9 House

◥ Viewpoint on photograph

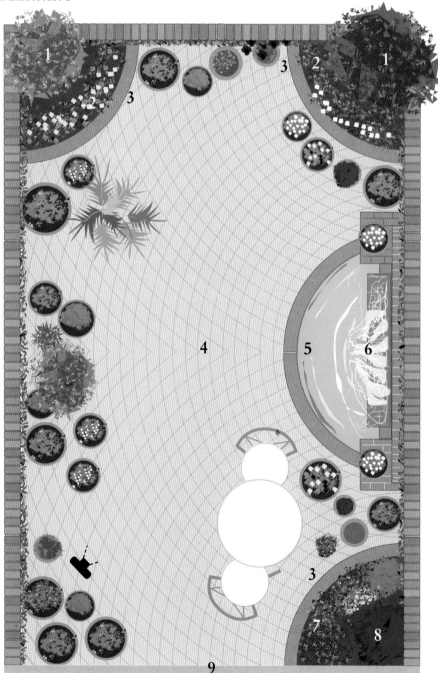

Circular themes can make use of full circles or crescents and arcs, sometimes overlapping as shown here. The three corner beds make use of quadrants. There's a sense of symmetry about this kind of garden, but simple mirror images could make it a little too predictable, and another cascade opposite this one would probably detract from the impact. The sound of two tumbling sheets of water might also cross the threshold between being pleasant and irritating.

Although there are plenty of pots in this design, little other maintenance is required so it is not especially labour-intensive. Pots of seasonal plants help to provide that vital dash of colour.

The choice of paving and the bricks used for the raised beds is also important in a garden like this. Here colours and textures have been chosen that blend together well, but if bricks and paving had been chosen with colours that did not harmonize, the overall effect might have been much less pleasing.

PLANTING

■ RIGHT

WALL MASKS AND SPOUTS

This kind of cascade is really a job for a professional or very experienced amateur, but it is possible to create a water spout on a more modest scale.

A high wall isn't necessary, as a gentle flow with a drop of 60–90cm (2–3ft) may sound more musical than a torrent from a high spout. Unless the feature is large, a low-voltage pump should be adequate, but choose one with a flow adjuster so that you have more control.

Metal pipework can be used, but plastic pipes are perfectly adequate. The difficulty lies in concealing pipes. Whenever possible, drill a hole through the wall and run the pipework up the back, bringing it back through the wall at the appropriate height. Disguise any unsightly pipes with an evergreen climber, such as ivy.

CROSS-SECTION OF A WALL MASK OR SPOUT

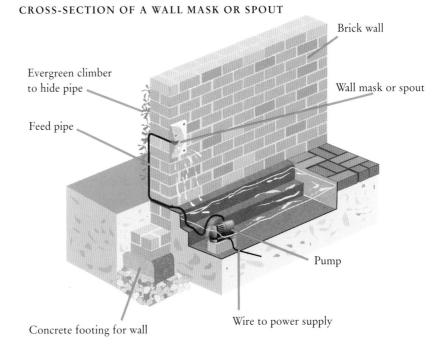

Brick wall

Evergreen climber to hide pipe

Wall mask or spout

Feed pipe

Pump

Concrete footing for wall

Wire to power supply

Planning and Planting

CLASSIC ROMANCE

With a little imagination you can bring a dream garden with classic connotations to life, even in a small town garden. All you need are some materials from a company specializing in reclaimed demolition materials and a vivid imagination.

PLANNING

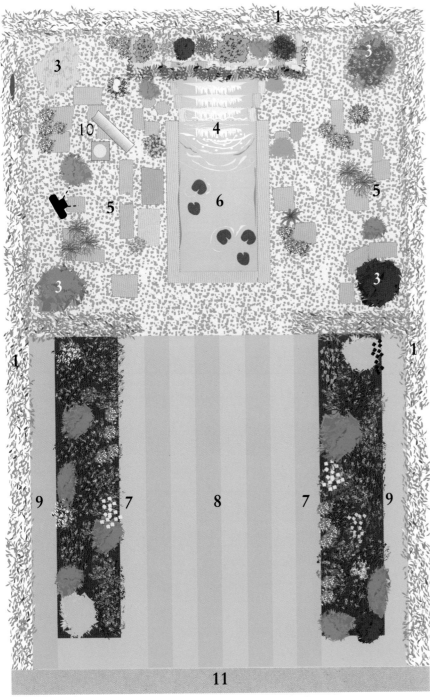

This is a garden for the romantic with a love of traditional gardens and a classical style. The "staircase" cascade forms the focal point, and it sets the tone for this part of the garden. Because it has been constructed mainly from reclaimed building materials from old houses, it has a timeless quality that can transform a town garden into a romantic piece of the past. The clever use of an old pillar, positioned so that it looks as though it fell from its pedestal many years ago, creates a wonderful sense of atmosphere.

Good old-fashioned herbaceous borders flanking the lawn reflect a formal style of gardening once popular, and the traditional yew hedges hold the two parts of the garden together.

When using reclaimed materials, it's best to have a flexible approach. Be prepared to modify your plans according to the materials you can obtain.

PLANTING

■ BELOW
CONSTRUCTING WATER STAIRS
The actual method of construction will depend on the materials used and the size of the feature, but the same principles can be applied to most forms of water stairs.

After excavating the pond area, form a consolidated slope of soil at an appropriate angle, taking into account the height of each step. On a natural slope you may only have to cut into the bank;

on a flat site it will be necessary to build it up and compact the ground.

Lay the pond liner first. Then lay a sheet of liner along the slope, leaving enough material to fold up at the sides to ensure a watertight channel. Use a liner underlay to protect it from stones, and it is worth using an extra layer of liner as access, for repairs will be difficult once construction is finished.

Lay a concrete pad on the bottom of the pond to support the brick wall. Place

a piece of spare liner over the bottom of the pond, folded over a couple of times, then construct a brick support wall to the height of the first riser.

Bed the first step on mortar, ensuring it has a slight slope forwards, but is level from left to right. Lay each of the other steps in the same way. At the top, make a chamber a couple of bricks high into which the return hose can be fed. Cover this with another slab or stone.

Ensure the liner comes up to the level of each step at the sides – it will be necessary to trim it to size. Be careful not to trim too short, and if possible leave it long enough to tuck into the soil mounded against each side. Plant lavishly with evergreens to hide the edges and any trace of the liner.

Once the mortar is completely dried, connect the pump and check for any leaks. A powerful pump will be required to ensure a fast flow of water over the edge of each lip. Consult an aquatic specialist for advice about the flow requirements before you buy. Also check on hose sizes and fittings. If in doubt, go for a larger size, as you can always turn down the flow if necessary.

CROSS-SECTION OF WATER STAIRS

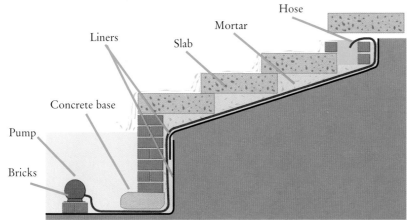

Hose

Mortar

Slab

Liners

Concrete base

Pump

Bricks

THE JAPANESE INFLUENCE

Authentic Japanese gardens are constructed according to strict rules, and features carry a significance that is seldom appreciated by Westerners. This in no way detracts from our ability to enjoy the style and aesthetics, and to incorporate some Japanese features into our own gardens, even if they lack the underlying significance of "authentic" Japanese gardening.

Whole books are written on the subject of Japanese gardening, but most of our designs seek only to capture the mood. Gardens have to be adapted to suit the environment and culture in which they are built. In our Western gardens, we may wish to introduce the Japanese influence only into part of our garden, or use a few key features as garden ornaments. Japanese votive lanterns, for example, are widely bought and positioned without regard to their original significance and are enjoyed purely as attractive garden ornaments. On the other hand, an area set aside as a Japanese-style garden will have a sense of peace and tranquillity that's special and supremely relaxing. Even if you are not persuaded to convert the whole of your garden, a Japanese corner will certainly add grace and elegance.

■ ABOVE
A simple feature like this evokes images of Japanese culture.

■ OPPOSITE
A Western interpretation of the style, using Japanese features and plants.

INSPIRATIONAL IDEAS

Japanese influences can be introduced to your garden in varying degrees. You won't have to completely redesign your garden for it to take on an oriental air. A quiet pool, rocks, or lanterns can all add to the effect if chosen and positioned with care.

■ OPPOSITE

The space at the side of a town house is often neglected because it's so difficult to persuade plants to thrive there, and the scope for a strong design is severely limited. This design shows how Japanese images and features can be put to good use in a most unpromising position. Note the stone steps and the use of large, smooth boulders amongst the gravel and shrubs.

■ BELOW

Although there are Japanese influences in the water garden, this is clearly a hybrid with a more traditional Western style. For many gardens, this may work better than a stricter interpretation of the Japanese style.

■ BELOW

A garden like this won't demand much maintenance, other than clipping the domes two or three times a year, yet it has as much impact as one packed with flowers. This genuine Japanese garden, combining water, rocks and carefully chosen shrubs, may not be to the taste of gardeners more used to a rainbow of colour, but it has a different function.

Know-how

STEPS AND STONES

The starkness of Japanese-style gardens may be unappealing to gardeners who expect to see greenery and colourful blooms, but the appeal of natural materials such as stones and bamboo compensates with a serene style, as can be seen in these very different gardens.

■ LEFT
This is typical of a garden where elements of Japanese gardening have been mixed with normal Western elements. Imaginative use of large stone slabs and gravel has created two paths leading down the garden, and the beds on either side are bordered with bamboo fencing.

■ BELOW
In a small garden it may be possible to devote only a corner to a collection of Japanese images. This inevitably means compromise, but the message is clearly received even in this small corner. A combination of rocks, stones and gravel provides the perfect setting for the shrubs, and the look is complemented by the attractive bamboo fence and the white-painted wall, which together provide a background that doesn't detract from the effect.

■ OPPOSITE
Though created far from Japan, this garden shows strong oriental influences. A wide path of small stones, inset with square stepping stones, is lined with informally planted beds. At the end are some specimen plants in decorative pots. The surrounding fences and buildings have been cleverly masked with reed screens to enhance the oriental feeling.

Know-how
WATER FEATURES

Ponds, lakes and streams form the heart of many large Japanese gardens, but in a small garden the scope for these may be limited.

Fortunately, water is used in many other ways, most of which can be incorporated into even a modest-sized garden.

■ LEFT
DISPLAY PLATFORMS You can make a small pond look oriental if it's accompanied by suitable bridges and rocks. Here, a couple of charming bonsai, displayed on a platform that reflects the materials and style of the bridge, bring out the essential "Japanese" ambience.
DESIGN TIP *Don't use rocks only around the edge of the pond. Try to position a few rocks in the water as well. Try covering them with moss and perhaps planting a bonsai in a suitable crevice. Be careful not to puncture the liner (use pieces of off-cuts beneath the rocks), and don't forget that your bonsai will still require regular watering despite being surrounded by water.*

■ RIGHT
WATER BASIN
Water basins capture the essence of a Japanese garden, and are small enough to feature in any garden. Traditionally, the water is fed through a bamboo flume.
DESIGN TIP *Don't be tempted to elevate the basin higher than suggested by the manufacturer. The low-level placement is symbolic, requiring a low stooping position to use it, as a gesture of humility for the ritual cleansing before the tea ceremony.*

■ LEFT

BRIDGES Water provides an ideal excuse for including a wonderful Japanese bridge, bright red being the usual colour. These are focal points in their own right, but also cast enchanting reflections.

DESIGN TIP *Whether making the bridge or buying it, it makes sense to span the narrowest part of the pond or stream. If necessary, just make a small inlet that extends a little way past the bridge to give the illusion that the water flows beyond.*

PUMPS

Most small water features, such as deer scarers and water basins, require only a very gentle flow of water. An inexpensive, small, low-voltage pump is adequate, and this can be housed in a small hidden reservoir beneath the feature, water trickling through pebbles supported on a strong mesh base, to be recirculated.

■ RIGHT

ORNAMENTS This large pond benefits from this focal point. Ornaments should be simple but striking, and have relevance to the scene.

DESIGN TIP *Don't overdo the ornaments, especially if you have used lanterns around the garden. Too many focal points will clash with each other. A few striking features usually work better than many mediocre focal points.*

Know-how

ROCK AND STONE

From early times, the Japanese have had a deep and abiding affinity with rock. Rock forms an important element in their landscape, and it symbolizes durability. It is possible to construct a Japanese garden without rocks, but it would be a pity not to include this most attractive of materials.

■ BELOW
CHOOSING ROCKS Consider colour, texture and size when choosing rocks. Here the different surfaces and sizes look as though they have been deposited naturally beside the stream.
DESIGN TIP *Random positioning of rocks and pebbles will create a natural look, enhanced by clusters of water plants.*

■ ABOVE
LARGE ROCKS
A couple of large rocks have transformally dull corner of this Japanese garden. Whether you view them as symbols or simply as an ornament, they are a striking focal point and make a feature of a part of the garden that would otherwise go almost unnoticed.
DESIGN TIP
Rocks like this are heavy to move. To help get the positioning right without too many attempts, make a number of sketches to show the selected rocks in a number of positions. Begin to position them only when you have a sketch that looks convincing.

■ BELOW

FEATURE FOUNTAIN A drilled boulder through which water is pumped so that it trickles gently over the surface creates a wonderfully calming and refreshing feature, especially on a hot day. By surrounding it with gravel topped with smaller boulders or beach pebbles a rock landscape is achieved. Adding a few other large rocks ensures this looks more like an erupting volcanic island set among a sea of pebbles.

DESIGN TIP *A feature like this can form part of a larger Japanese garden, but it would also make a pleasing water feature in another style of garden, to bring interest to an otherwise dull corner, perhaps where plants struggle to thrive.*

■ ABOVE

PATHWAYS Rocks with a suitably flat surface are sometimes used as stepping stones – through either lawn or water. They form a path that leads you through the garden, and the size and spacing of the stones are specially selected and positioned to dictate the pace at which you make the journey.

DESIGN TIP *Stepping stones placed close together slow up the speed of travel. Wider spacing will tend to speed up the pace. You can use different spacing to determine the rate at which the garden is to be explored, or vary the pace to meet the needs of different parts of the garden, perhaps dwelling on a feature of which you are specially proud.*

BUYING ROCK AND STONE

Garden centres and builders' merchants are likely to stock only a limited range or rocks and stones. Look in local directories for stone merchants – these should have a reasonable selection.

For a large feature it may be best to visit a suitable quarry, and perhaps select your rocks there. However, bear in mind that carriage is substantial on such a heavy material, so if possible use a local rock rather than one found perhaps in another part of the country, to save on carriage.

Know-how

SAND AND GRAVEL

Dry landscapes, with the emphasis on the element of stone, have their origins in the Zen style of gardening, its history originating from a form of Buddhism. This is a fascinating garden form to explore in specialist books on the subject, but you can imitate some of the elements in your own garden without an in-depth knowledge of the symbolism.

■ LEFT
GRAVEL OR SAND CIRCLES
Long straight lines of raked gravel or sand usually suggest calm water, and wavy lines evoke flowing water. Concentric circles in gravel also imply a sense of movement, perhaps where the water flows around an "island".
DESIGN TIP *To prevent gravel spilling over on to beds, borders, lawns or paths and ruining the design, it is important to have a firm, raised edge to a dry garden whenever possible.*

■ RIGHT
GRAVEL LINES
Where space is limited, a Japanese-style garden can be achieved by combining raked sand, rock and boulders and lantern in a vacant corner. The bridge here is for aesthetic purposes, rather than for practical reasons.
DESIGN TIP *Be cautious about using raked sand or gravel close to deciduous trees. Maintaining this neat appearance will be far from easy in autumn.*

■ ABOVE

COMPLEMENTING GRAVEL
The area of raked gravel or sand is usually limited, and here the path in
the foreground is created from flat
rounded stones, toning in with the
almost mountain scree landscape of
the rocks beside it.
DESIGN TIP *Be cautious about raked
gravel where it might be used as a path or
short-cut – it only takes one pair of feet to
ruin the effect! Here a paved area has
been provided around the edge to avoid
this risk and provide a pleasing contrast.*

■ RIGHT

DRY BRIDGES Bridges can be built
over dry garden "rivers" and "cascades",
but these may spoil the scale of the
landscape unless used with care.
DESIGN TIP *Dry gardens are striking
features, but they can look a little barren
to Western eyes. Plenty of plants in the
background will help.*

Planning and Planting

STONE AND WATER

Two elements of symbolic importance in Japanese gardens are stone and water, both of which feature strongly in this design. This is a garden for contemplation and quiet admira-tion – not a family garden for children to play in. It's important to have a clear idea of what you want from this style, and to modify the degree of authenticity to suit.

PLANNING

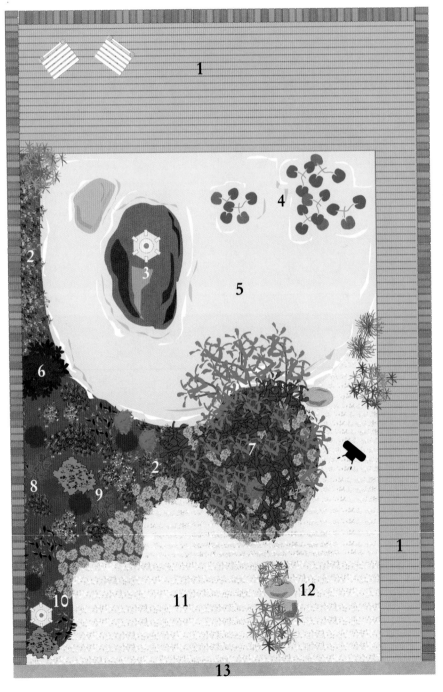

KEY TO PLAN

1 Timber decking
2 Mat-forming ground cover
3 Rock island with lantern
4 Water lilies
5 Pond
6 Specimen shrub
7 Specimen tree
8 Climber on wall
9 Dwarf shrubs
10 Japanese lantern
11 Raked gravel
12 Rocks and bamboo
13 House

➤ Viewpoint on photograph

This stylish Japanese garden makes extensive use of raked gravel, with rock "islands" and associated plants. In our plan, extensive use has also been made of water, another very pleasing visual and aural element that features strong-ly in the Japanese style of garden-ing. Plants have been used to cre-ate shapes and textures, and foliage effect is more important than colourful flowers. Before setting to work on this kind of garden, it's worth spending time doing some in-depth reading on Japanese gar-dens and their symbolism.

Although raked gravel is a very visual device, and highly attractive, you should bear in mind that the family dog and local wildlife or playful children will quickly make

PLANTING

re-raking an urgent priority if you are to keep it looking good. In addition, the area will require regular clearing and raking during the autumn to remove fallen leaves.

UNDERSTANDING LANTERNS

Japanese lanterns make a fascinating study worth reading up on or sending for catalogues from specialist suppliers. Their form and function are steeped in ancient conventions and traditions. In the mean time, it might be helpful to understand some of the basic terms: the parts of the lantern, the variety of styles and how the lantern should be positioned in relation to the house, if you want to be precise.

■ RIGHT

Lanterns may not have all the six parts illustrated here. The base may also be described as legs, pedestal or earth ring; the pillar called the trunk or shaft; and the roof referred to as the umbrella.

POSITIONING LANTERNS

■ ABOVE

Although most Western gardeners simply position their lanterns where they look pleasing, they should be angled towards a point where the centreline meets the house, as shown in the illustration.

THE PARTS OF A LANTERN

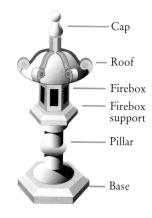

- Cap
- Roof
- Firebox
- Firebox support
- Pillar
- Base

KNOW YOUR STYLES

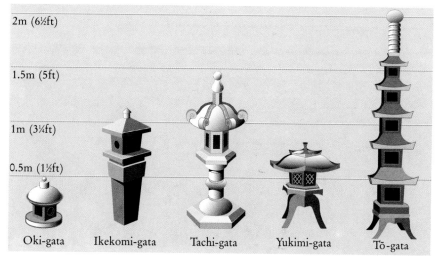

2m (6½ft)

1.5m (5ft)

1m (3¼ft)

0.5m (1½ft)

Oki-gata   Ikekomi-gata   Tachi-gata   Yukimi-gata   Tō-gata

Planning and Planting

A GARDEN OF ELEMENTS

Symbolism is important in a Japanese garden, and here rock, water and wood, all strong forces in nature, help to give this garden strong imagery.

PLANNING

Because many features in Japanese gardens, such as water, rock and gravel mingled with plants, are designed to be viewed rather than sat among, it's important to provide suitable viewing areas. Decking blends in unobtrusively, and here it has been used on three sides to provide ample viewing angles as well as somewhere to sit and entertain.

A water feature like this, with a combination of rectangles and curves, and rocks placed within the pond, makes construction difficult for an amateur. It is worth taking professional advice when thinking about a creating a water feature of this size and complexity. Positioning heavy rocks also calls for teamwork.

DECIDING ON DECKING
Complicated decks with several changes in level or which project over water, for example, as here, require special construction techniques. There are companies who specialize in making and installing decking, and these should be consulted if you are in any doubt.

KEY TO PLAN

1 Bamboo screen
2 Climbers
3 Mound-forming plants
4 Bamboos
5 Japanese lantern
6 Rocks
7 Pebbles and gravel
8 Pond
9 Water irises
10 Timber decking
11 Dwarf shrubs
12 House

🎏 Viewpoint on photograph

PLANTING

HOW TO MAKE SIMPLE DECKING

1 Level the area to be decked, then position bricks or blocks on which the bearers will be supported. Bearers must be clear of the ground so that they are not in contact with damp earth and to allow air to circulate freely beneath the decking. If the ground is unstable, set the bricks or blocks on pads of concrete. Make sure they are level, or the final decking will not be stable.

2 Apply an additional coat of preservative to all fence posts. Lay out the posts provisionally, to check that the supports are spaced closely enough together and to ensure that they are cut so that two lengths butt over a support block. Lay heavy-duty polythene (plastic) over the ground to prevent weeds growing through. Water will drain away where the sheets overlap.

3 Lay the posts over a waterproof membrane where they come into contact with the supporting bricks, and ensure that any joins are positioned over the support. Cut gravel boards to size and coat with preservative. Fix these to the posts using galvanized nails. Leave a gap of about 6mm (¼in) between each board to allow water to drain and the wood to swell safely.

Planning and Planting

SHADES OF GREY AND GREEN

Japanese-style gardens make their statements in a more subtle way than many of us are used to, often to stunning effect. Rocks like grey granite and grey gravel and pebbles have a bold yet restrained visual impact, and make a wonderful backdrop for the many shades of green foliage.

PLANNING

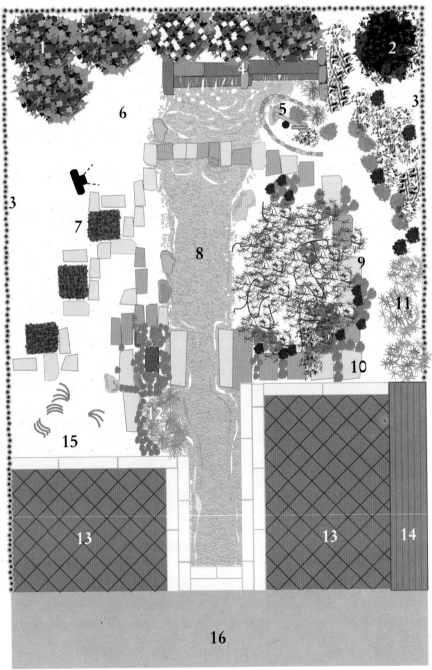

KEY TO PLAN

1 Rhododendron banks
2 Specimen tree
3 Bamboo fence
4 Granite retaining wall incorporating cascade
5 Deer scarer
6 Gravel
7 Clipped box squares
8 Stream with gravel bed
9 Pine tree with ground cover beneath
10 Stepping stones set into gravel
11 Bamboos
12 Dwarf rushes
13 Patio
14 Tea house
15 Terracotta tiles vertically embedded into gravel
16 House

Viewpoint on photograph

Water and rock play their usual important roles in this design, with the "stream" that runs the length of the garden being the central feature and holding the garden together. It draws the eye inward rather than to the boundaries, and the uncluttered open space generates an impression of size in a limited space. These are qualities that make the Japanese style suitable for gardens of all sizes, even small ones.

For a design like this to work properly, it's important to use appropriate materials. It is advisable to have a complex and possibly expensive garden like this constructed professionally, or at least take the advice of specialist suppliers before you start.

PLANTING

■ RIGHT

EASY-TO-MAKE TEA HOUSE This professional-looking tea house was made by an amateur from inexpensive and scrap wood, and shows what can be achieved with a little imagination and enthusiasm.

The side panels were made from a sheet of white material secured behind a home-made trellis constructed from battens, and the other walls were constructed from scrap timber. To give an attractive appearance and to admit light on the inside, rolls of tied reeds were secured in position. The roof "tiles" are easy to make from feather-edged fencing boards, and the flashing around the finial at the top makes it weatherproof. As the wind can swirl into the open front, it is important with this kind of structure to secure the upright posts well into the ground. The seat was made from old railway sleepers (railroad ties), supported on short off-cuts of the same material. A black wood preservative on the exterior timber ensures this home-made structure has a really professional and authentic finish. Although the detailed construction of this kind of feature depends on the materials available, it shows what an excellent project a tea house makes for a do-it-yourself enthusiast.

Planning and Planting
MERGING WITH NATURE

Japanese gardens often reflect the natural world and its forces symbolically, but traditionally Japanese gardens are often designed to give a spectacular natural view from a vantage point, perhaps glimpsed as one bends down at a water basin. This garden simply becomes part of the landscape, natural and man-made merging almost imperceptibly. The large pond is a striking central feature, but will need regular care and maintenance to keep it looking its best.

KEY TO PLAN

1 To open countryside
2 Bamboo hedge
3 Ornamental grasses and wild plants
4 Timber decking pontoon
5 Pond
6 Bog plants
7 Grasses and sedges
8 Marginal pond plants
9 Japanese lantern on pedestal
10 Bamboo water spout
11 Planted containers
12 Paving of granite setts
13 Gravel
14 House
   Viewpoint on photograph

PLANNING

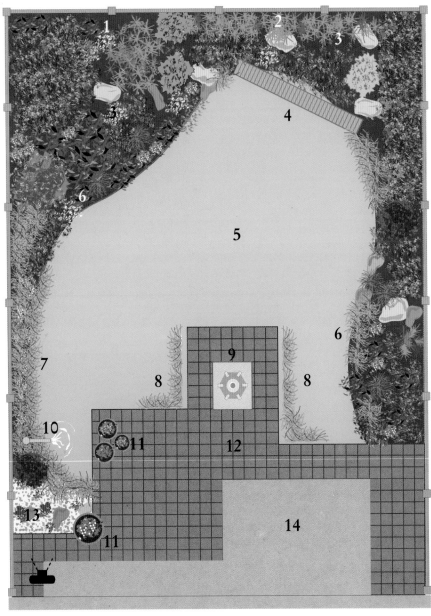

This garden almost merges with the landscape, but the mountains in the distance are in Switzerland, not Japan. Wherever there's a superb view, this kind of garden should appeal.

The whole garden revolves around the pond, the banks of which provide an opportunity for growing plenty of bog plants, blended with grasses and wild plants further back. This enables the garden to merge into the natural setting beyond, with no clear boundary when viewed from the house.

The more structured part of the garden, with its hard edges and rigid shapes, is confined to the area immediately outside the house. It is from this part of the garden that the view will be enjoyed, surrounded by the sights and sounds of nature. The bamboo spout adds to the musical sounds associated with water.

■ RIGHT

HOW TO MAKE A BAMBOO WATER SPOUT

A water spout is quite easy to make. You may find it difficult to obtain lengths of bamboo of suitable thickness, but you can buy the spouts ready-made.

Buy a small plastic or glass-fibre reservoir, and sink this into the ground, a little below surface level. Place a small low-voltage pump in the reservoir, standing it on a brick to reduce the risk of the filter clogging with debris. Cover with a piece of strong metal mesh, larger than the reservoir.

Fix a length of flexible hose to the outlet of the pump, long enough to feed through the bamboo. Hollow out the bamboo if necessary, and cut a hole in the upright piece large enough to take the spout as a tight fit. Secure with a waterproof adhesive, then bind and tie black twine around the joint. Thread the hose through the spout and down the main stem, making sure it does not show. Then secure the bottom of the hose to the pump with steel hose clamps.

Fill the reservoir, then test. It may be necessary to adjust the flow with a valve fitted to the pump – a gentle trickle is often more effective than a torrent. Make sure the water is not thrown beyond the reservoir. If it is, reduce the flow or lay pond liner around the area with the edge covered to channel the water back into the tank.

Cover the strong metal mesh with large pebbles completely. Heap up pebbles around the base of the bamboo to keep it stable.

As water will be lost through evaporation and splashes blown in the wind, check the reservoir periodically. The level must always cover the pump. Use a dipstick to tell you when it requires topping up without having to remove all the pebbles.

WATER PUMP

Decorative binding

Flexible hose from pump

Hollowed bamboo

Layer of pebbles to conceal mesh

Cable to transformer

Metal mesh overlapping edge

Low-voltage pump on brick

Plastic or glass-fibre reservoir

Waterproof connnector

PLANTING

Planning and Planting
FORCES OF NATURE

This oriental garden uses the dramatic landscape of rock banks and forceful cascades, as you might find on a wild mountainside, offset by an area of gravel traversed by a meandering stepping-stone path.

PLANNING

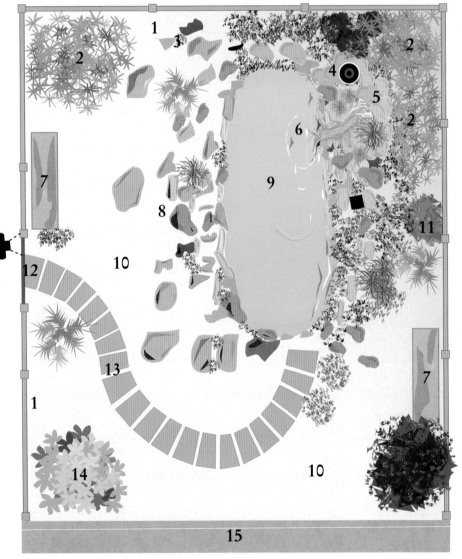

To introduce a sense of calm to the rest of the garden, a large area of gravel has been used, together with restrained planting with bamboos and Japanese acers (maples) in key focal points.

ALONG THE GARDEN PATH
Paths in Japanese gardens tend to meander rather than lead in straight lines by the shortest route. Stepping stones are popular, as they affect the pace at which you proceed through the garden, as well as adding so much more character than ordinary paving slabs. These are a few ideas for stepping-stone paths.

When choosing stepping stones, an irregular shape is often more appealing than rectangular slabs of stone, but in the interests of safety try to ensure the actual stepping surface is reasonably flat and even.

Rock features like the one shown here are difficult and expensive to construct, and professional assistance will probably be required, but the effect is stunning by day and enchanting at night if the cas-cades are illuminated. A pond as large as this will also suit fish such as koi, which bring their own fascinating charm as they come up to feed. They also emphasize the Japanese theme.

PLANTING

STEPPING-STONE PATHS

■ ABOVE
Reasonably flat and evenly spaced stones make this an easy path to traverse, but these stones and the curve form an essential part of the design of the garden, and are much more interesting than a strictly functional garden path.

■ ABOVE
These stones project high above the surrounding ground and are irregularly spaced. Exploring this path, which is heavily planted on each side, is a more adventurous experience. It suggests a journey down a river full of obstacles, with dark and mysterious banks.

■ ABOVE
These stepping stones lead enticingly through a border of small shrubs, crossing a ribbon of pebbles that suggest a dried-up river bed. This use of paths makes even a short and simple journey to the bottom of the garden an exciting experience.

MAINTAING A WATER GARDEN

Adding a water feature to your garden will undoubtedly enhance its aesthetic appeal, but you will need to carry out a number of tasks in order to keep it looking its very best. If you have a pond, you will also need to decide on what plants to include, finding an attractive balance between bog plants, marginals and deep-water plants. Beware of concentrating solely on more showy species of water plant. Water lilies are undeniably beautiful, but your pond will also need other floating water plants and oxygenators to keep it in good health. In addition, it is important to keep a vigilant eye on the water level during particularly arid summers, and top up when required. Check for water clarity and remain ever watchful for weeds and pests that could blight your pond. Once you have decided what to stock your pool with, this section looks at how to establish water plants, from bog plants to surface floaters and water lilies.

■ ABOVE
This bog iris being removed from the edge of the pond for propagation.

■ OPPOSITE
Large ponds like this one require a considerable amount of work to keep them looking their best all year round.

STOCKING THE POOL

When deciding what to plant, you need to strike a good balance between bog plants, marginals and deep-water plants; you should also include oxygenators and floating water plants. All pond stocking is best done in spring when there is less danger of freezing temperatures.

Always buy plants from a reputable source. Check for any signs of blanketweed, duckweed or water snails. If the plant pot feels at all slimy, reject it. It is difficult to keep the water entirely free of water snails or pond weeds, but don't go out of your way to encourage them.

Bog plants can be planted directly into the moist soil surrounding a natural pond, or by a stream, or in an artificial bog garden. You can also grow them in pots on the shelves of the pond, but you may need to raise them on bricks to keep the crowns above water level. If growing them in this way, use ordinary pots, plastic or terracotta, not the baskets that are often sold for water plants.

Unless you have a natural stream or very large pond, most marginals and deep-water plants are best grown in containers to restrict their spread. For marginals you can use conventional pots or aquatic planting baskets;

deep-water plants are best in baskets. Choose a basket with a fine mesh, so that lining is unnecessary.

Use ordinary garden soil in the containers or compost (soil mix) specially formulated for aquatic plants. The soil should not be too rich as excessive nutrients will leach out into the water and encourage algal growth.

Most marginals need about 7.5–15cm (3–6in) of water

above their crowns, so you may need to stand pots on bricks to ensure the correct planting depth. Calculate the water depth by measuring from the top of the pot.

Young specimens of potentially large, deep-water plants should be planted shallowly to begin with. When planting a young water lily, for instance, make sure that the juvenile leaves float on the surface. As the plant grows and the stems extend, you can gradually lower it until you achieve the final planting depth.

Oxygenating plants and surface floaters do not need to be planted but simply introduced into the pool.

■ ABOVE
To plant an oxygenating water plant, such as the *Lagarosiphon major* (syn. *Elodea crispa*) shown here, tie it to a stone and then drop it in the water. The plant will root in the mud at the bottom of the pool.

■ ABOVE
Surface floaters succeed best in ponds with a good balance of plant material which supports a wide range of wildlife. In such a pond, the constant supply of droppings and other waste matter keeps the water rich in minerals.

PLANTING A BOG PLANT

Prepare the site well by forking it over and removing any perennial weeds such as couch grass. Boggy soil naturally retains fertility. Unless you know the soil is poor do not introduce bulky organic matter. This might lead to an excessive build-up of moisture that could damage plant tissue if it freezes in winter.

1 Dig a hole that is large enough to accommodate the plant.

2 Remove the plant from its container and place in the the hole.

3 Firm the plant in gently with your hands then water it well.

PLANTING A WATER LILY

1 Half fill an aquatic planting basket with ordinary garden soil. Place the water lily rhizome on top and continue to fill with soil.

2 Place stones or gravel on the surface to prevent the soil escaping from the basket and to reduce the risk of fish stirring up the mud.

3 Flood the basket with water, then gently lower it into the pool to the appropriate depth.

ROUTINE POND MAINTENANCE

Although informal ponds tend to look after themselves, you can help promote a healthy balance of plants and encourage other species to inhabit the pond. Check the water level and keep an eye out for leaks. Keeping the water clear of algae and other invasive plants will give the pond's other inhabitants the best possible chance to thrive.

MAINTAINING THE WATER LEVEL

You will need to fill up the water in the pond periodically, particularly in summer. Allowing the level to drop too much may expose the liner to the potentially harmful rays of the sun. Fill the pond in the evening with a hose. If you can raise the end of the hose above the water level, the resultant agitation will help to oxygenate the water and will be beneficial to any fish in the pond.

■ ABOVE
As the water evaporates, particularly in summer, use a garden hose to top up.

CHECKING FOR LEAKS

Some gardeners like to drain and refill the pond annually, although this is not a good idea if you keep fish, while others do it every two or three years. However, it is only necessary to drain a pond if a leak develops in the liner. The tell-tale sign that there is a leak is a dramatic drop in the water level, but before you drain the pond, check the edges to make sure that the liner has not collapsed at any point. If part of the liner has slipped below the desired water level, build it up again from behind, then fill the pond with fresh water.

If you are sure there is a leak, press all around the liner with your hands to locate it (the soil behind the hole will feel soft and boggy), then drain the pond to below the level of the leak. You will then need to repair the liner, using a repair kit appropriate to the type of liner material.

■ ABOVE
When oxygenating plants become congested, lift out clumps with your hands and tear them apart, returning about half to two-thirds to the water.

KEEPING THE WATER CLEAR

Most informal ponds are self-maintaining once the balance of plant and insect life is established, and you should have no major problems with water clarity.

Algal growth sometimes develops in spring and summer, however, where water lilies and other plants with floating leaves are not mature enough to cover the required area (between 50 and 70 per cent of the water surface).

The problem may also be due to an insufficiency of oxygenating plants, but if the pond is a new one, or if you have just replaced all the water, it usually clears of its own accord. Otherwise, check the pool for dead or decaying leaves and flowers, and remove them. To clear the water quickly, use an ultraviolet clarifier.

In a formal pool where the water itself is the focal point, eliminating algae may require more regular intervention. It is easier to keep a large pool clear than a small one. You can keep the water clear in a variety of ways. If the pool supports no plants or wildlife whatsoever, you can add any proprietary cleaning agent such as the chlorine that is usually used in swimming pools. If you keep fish in a pond with plants, add an ultraviolet clarifier to keep the water clear.

POND WEEDS

Blanketweed (*Spirogyra*) is a plant that grows beneath the water surface in dense strands and is most prevalent during warm weather. You may not realize you have it until it comes to the surface, where it forms unsightly masses. It is easy to remove with a long cane, and makes good composting material.

In summer you may also notice duckweed (*Lemna*), a tiny two-leaved plant with roots that trail in the water. Remove immediately with a net, as it spreads rapidly.

From time to time, thin oxygenating plants by pulling out clumps with your hands, leaving enough behind to ensure water clarity. Thin little and often.

WATER SNAILS

Water snails can be a problem, since they feed on plants and nibble away at the undersides of water lily leaves. A few will not do any significant harm, and may even help to control blanketweed, but you can reduce their numbers by floating a lettuce leaf on the surface of the water and leaving it overnight. Next morning, lift the leaf and dispose of any water snails that have accumulated there. The ramshorn snail, however, is a beneficial mollusc since it feeds on decaying matter at the bottom of the pond.

■ ABOVE
If you leave a lettuce leaf on the surface of the water overnight, it will trap water snails. You can then dispose of them the following morning.

■ LEFT
This duckweed should be removed before it has a chance to spread. It is very hardy and spreads so quickly that you need to check for it regularly.

THE POND IN WINTER

A few end-of-season tasks are essential if you want your pond, and its plants and fish, to remain in good condition. These include keeping the water clear of leaves and other debris, and lifting and dividing any overgrown plants. The pump, too, may need attention now: if you leave a pump in your pond in shallow water over winter, ice may damage it. Once the pump is out of the water, have it serviced if necessary so that it will be ready for use in spring.

PROTECTING POND PUMPS

1 Remove submersible pumps before frosts cause the water to freeze deeply, unless it is below the ice line and needed to sustain a biological filter, which some people prefer to keep working.

2 Clean the pump thoroughly before you put it away. It will probably be covered in algae, which can be scrubbed off with a stiff brush.

3 Remove the filter and either replace it with a new one or clean it.

4 Make sure all the water is drained from the pump. If your pump is an external one, drain the system.

5 Read the manufacturer's instructions, and carry out any other servicing that is necessary before storing the pump in a dry place. If you need to send the pump away for a service, do it now instead of waiting until the following spring.

CARING FOR THE POND IN WINTER

1 Protect the pond from the worst of the leaf fall with a fine-mesh net or rake to remove leaves. Concentrate not only on the surface but also the deeper water.

2 Submerged oxygenating plants will eventually clog the pond unless you net or rake them out periodically. Thin them by raking out the excess.

3 Trim back any dead or dying plants, especially where the vegetation is likely to fall into the water.

4 To divide overgrown water plants, first remove the plants from their containers. It may be necessary to cut some roots to do so.

5 Some plants can be pulled apart by hand, but you may find some too tangled and have to chop them into smaller pieces with a spade.

6 Pot up pieces of plants in planting baskets. Cover the surface of the basket with gravel to prevent the soil being washed away.

7 Some aquatic plants may be killed by frost. Net a few plants that are in good condition (see left). Keep the plants in a warm, light place, such as a greenhouse or conservatory. You might also be able to keep them on a light windowsill. Top up or change the water occasionally to prevent the water becoming stagnant (see right).

PROPAGATION

Such is the diversity of water plants that a number of methods of propagation can be used. The ones detailed below are those generally practised and are suitable for most of the plants referred to in this book.

PROPAGATION BY DIVISION

To create new plants that are identical to the parent, you should propagate vegetatively. Division is the simplest method and is suitable for all bog plants that form clumps. It can be used both to increase stock and to thin out congested plants. Dig up the plants in spring or autumn and divide the clumps either by hand or with two garden forks, held back to back. Replant only the best pieces.

Plants that form a rhizome (a thick, modified underground stem) need to be cut into pieces (see Dividing a bog iris), as do water lilies (see Dividing a water lily).

Marginal plants grown in containers rapidly become congested and will need to be divided every other year or so.

■ ABOVE
After division, bog irises can be potted up in sections, either individually or in groups, and then returned to the pond.

DIVIDING A BOG IRIS

1 Lift the plant from the pond, and remove any stones from the surface of the basket.

2 If the roots have grown through the basket, as here, then cut the basket away with a sharp knife.

3 Open up the plant and cut through the rhizome. Make sure each section has a good root system.

4 Pull the plant apart with your hands in order to free the individual sections.

PROPAGATING BY SEED

If you wish to collect your own seed, allow the seedheads to develop on the plant after flowering. When dry, remove and shake the ripe seed on to a piece of paper. Sow at once or store in paper bags for sowing next spring.

Seed is usually available commercially from early spring until autumn, and the temperature for germination is given on the seed packet: some seeds need to be sown in warmth, others need a period of cold.

For the best results, use a proprietory, fine-textured seed compost (soil mix) that is low in nutrients. Protect summer and autumn sowings in a cold frame over winter; spring ones can be planted out in a nursery bed when large enough. Water well at all times.

1 Fill the base of a seed tray with stones for drainage. Fill the tray with seed compost (soil mix) to within about 1cm (1/2 in) of the top.

2 Firm down the compost (soil mix) gently with a tray. Do not compact the compost. Spray with water or stand the tray in shallow water until the surface is damp.

3 Scatter seed thinly and evenly on the surface, then cover with a fine layer of compost. Put the tray in a shaded place and spray regularly. When the seedlings are large enough to handle, pot up and grow on.

DIVIDING A WATER LILY

If a water lily has grown too large you need to divide it. You do not need to treat the cut surfaces but can simply replant them. If you wish merely to reduce the size of the plant, cut the rhizome in half, then pot up the pieces into aquatic baskets and return them to the pool. If your aim is to produce many new plants, cut small sections and grow them on in a wet environment, outside the pool, for a year before planting.

1 Lift the water lily in spring and remove all the soil. Trim back overlong roots and damaged leaves.

2 Cut the rhizome into pieces, making sure each section has roots and leaves or leaf buds.

3 Plant sections in pots containing ordinary garden soil, and top with gravel for protection.

4 Stand the pot in a bowl of water. After about a year, the plant can be returned to the pool.

PLANT DIRECTORY

There is a wealth of plants to choose from for planting in rock and water gardens. The plants described in this section should help you make a varied selection, whether you want to stock up a large pool or plant a raised bed.

WATER PLANTS

Choosing water plants can be bewildering, and you will find that there are always more desirable plants to grow than space available. For a balanced pond, it's important to include some

Hosta 'Tall Boy', like most other hostas, appreciates soil that does not dry out. Its tall lilac flowers will make a striking addition to any bog garden.

Lysichiton americanus, commonly known as skunk cabbage, is one of the most flamboyant of water plants. In summer, it produces an arsenal of large, yellow spathes.

submerged oxygenators as well as deep-water plants such as water lilies to provide vital foliage cover over part of the surface. However, it's among the marginal plants (those planted in shallow water at the edge) and bog plants for wet ground outside the pond that the greatest variety can be found.

WATER LILIES

It is important to select suitable varieties of water lily (*Nymphaea*) for the size of your pond. Some of the most vigorous ones are suitable only for lakes and very large

Nymphaea 'Gladstoneana' is a vigorous water lily for larger ponds. In summer, its large white flowers float on the surface. Grow in full sun and divide in spring.

ponds, whilst others are miniatures, suitable for water features in sinks and tubs. If in doubt, always check with your supplier. Good ones for a small pond are 'Candida' (white with yellow centres), 'Pink Opal' and

Nymphaea 'Attraction' is a moderately vigorous water lily suitable for a medium-sized pool. Its cup-shaped, crimson flowers form a star shape in summer.

'Laydeckeri Lilacina' (pink), 'Froebeli' (bright red), 'Pygmaea Helvola' (yellow) and 'Graziella' (apricot-yellow changing to crimson). For medium-sized ponds, suitable varieties include 'Hermine' and 'Gonnère' (white), 'Amabilis' and 'Firecrest' (pink), 'Attraction' and 'Laydeckeri Purpurata' (red), 'Marliacea chromatella'

Nymphaea 'Amabilis' is an attractive water lily, producing pink flowers that float on the surface of the water in summer. Grow in full sun and divide in spring.

(yellow) and 'Indiana' (orange-yellow changing to copper-red). For deep pools, choose from 'Gladstoneana' (white), 'Marliacea Carnea' and 'Pink Sensation' (pink), 'Escarboucle' (red), 'Sunrise' (yellow) and 'Comanche' (yellow changing to copper-red).

OTHER PLANTS FOR DEEP WATER
So-called deep-water plants are grown with about 30cm (1ft) or more of water above

Water crowfoot (*Ranunculus aquatilis*) has both floating and submerged leaves. In spring and summer, pure white, buttercup-like flowers appear above the water.

their crowns, although most will grow in water more than twice this depth. Water lilies are the best-known deep-water aquatics, but try the water hawthorn (*Aponogeton distachyos*), which has slightly fragrant, white flowers that bloom from spring to autumn. It can be rampant if planted directly in mud at the bottom of the pond, but is suitable for any pond if it is planted in a container. Another plant to consider is the yellow water lily (*Nuphar lutea*), which has leathery, oval leaves and bowl-shaped yellow flowers; small species such as *N. japonica* var. *variegata* are most suited to shallow ponds. Finally, water buttercup (*Ranunculus aquatilis*), which has small, white, buttercup-like flowers and kidney-shaped floating leaves, is best suited to large wildlife pools.

PLANTS FOR SHALLOW MARGINS
"Marginal" plants need less water above their crowns than deep-water aquatics. They are often planted on special marginal shelves around the edge of the pond, about 23cm (9in) below the water. Some marginals are valued just for their foliage; these include Japanese rush (*Acorus gramineus* 'Variegatus') (cream-striped leaves); the corkscrew rush

Acorus gramineus 'Variegatus' is a marginal water plant with grass-like tufts of leaves. These have creamy-white margins and provide interest around the pond in winter.

(*Juncus effusus* 'Spiralis') (corkscrew-like foliage); and sedges (foliage).

For flowers and decorative foliage, try the water plantain (*Alisma plantago-aquatica*) (rosy-white flowers and a rosette of leaves); the flowering rush (*Butomus umbellatus*) (reddish-white flowers and thin, dark, triangular leaves); marsh marigolds (*Caltha palustris*) (yellow flowers and heart-shaped leaves); *Houttuynia cordata* (white flowers and

Pickerel weed (*Pontederia cordata*) originates from North America. It bears striking purple-blue flowers in late summer above heart-shaped, glossy green leaves.

This water forget-me-not, *Myosotis scorpioides* 'Mermaid', is a marginal plant with bright blue flowers in summer that rise above hairy, spoon-shaped leaves.

heart-shaped leaves); *Iris laevigata* (blue flowers and sword-shaped leaves); water mint (*Mentha aquatica*) (lilac flowers and pungent leaves); *Mimulus guttatus* (yellow flower spikes); water forget-me-not (*Myosotis scorpioides*) (light blue flowers with yellow eyes); pickerel weed (*Pontederia cordata*) (soft blue flower spikes and heart-shaped leaves); brooklime (*Veronica beccabunga*) (blue flowers with white centres); and arum lily (*Zantedeschia*

Ligularia dentata 'Desdemona' (syn. *Senecio clivorum* 'Desdemona') produces orange, daisy-like flowers above purple leaves in mid-to late summer.

aethiopica) (large white flowers and arrow-shaped leaves).

One final plant to consider is reedmace. Most of the species grow too vigorously for a pond, but *Typha angustifolia*, with poker-like, brown flowerheads and narrow grey-green leaves, and *T. laxmannii*, a slightly dwarf version, are both suitable.

OXYGENATING PLANTS

Few of these submerged plants enhance the pond

The oxygenating water or willow moss (*Fontinalis antipyretica*) is a submerged aquatic moss with long, slender stems and small, dark green, oval-shaped leaves.

visually, but they are invaluable for the health of the pond if you keep fish. They increase the oxygen content of the water when the fish most need it, and by absorbing nutrients they may also help to control the algae that cause green water. *Lagarosiphon major* (also known as *Elodea crispa*) is one of the best known, but it's a rampant grower and

may have to be thinned out periodically. The water milfoils (*Myriophyllum*) are some of the most attractive oxygenators because much of their feathery growth rises above the surface: whorled milfoil (*M. verticillatum*) has long, branching stems, whilst parrot's feather (*M. aquaticum*) has soft stems of finely divided foliage. Others to consider are Canadian pondweed (*Elodea canadensis*), one of the finest oxygenators for garden ponds, and curled pondweed (*Potamogeton crispus*), whose narrow, stalkless leaves have seaweed-like edges.

FLOATING PLANTS

Like oxygenating plants, these aquatics are vital for the well-being of the pool because they reduce algae, and so keep the water clear. Because they lie on the surface of the water, rather

Water soldier (*Stratiotes aloides*) is a floating water plant with rosettes of erect, sword-shaped leaves. Usually submerged, they rise above the surface in the summer.

than being submerged, their leaves and flowers can also be appreciated. Try fairy moss (*Azolla caroliniana*), which has delicate, fern-like leaves that turn red in autumn; water soldier (*Stratiotes aloides*), which rises to the surface in summer and resembles floating pineapple tops; and water chestnut (*Trapa natans*), whose diamond-shaped leaves form rosettes floating on spongy leafy stalks; the spiny fruits can be stored in wet moss until spring.

BOG PLANTS

Bog plants grow in mud or wet soil that does not dry out, but is not permanently submerged. Some will also survive in normal border soil, but others will soon die if the ground dries out. Many primulas, such as *Primula japonica* and *P. bulleyana*, make excellent bog plants, and look their best when

Primula japonica, a bog plant from Japan, has eye-catching white, pink or magenta-red flowers from late spring to midsummer as well as bright green leaves.

Rheum palmatum originates from North-West China. Its modest appearance is brushed aside in early summer when panicles of vertiginous crimson flowers burst forth.

grown in groups. Other plants to choose from for spring flowering include bugle (*Ajuga reptans*) (blue flowers and dark green

Primula bulleyana, a bog plant from South-West China, bears showy orange flowers in early summer above dark green leaves. This plant can be grown in sun or shade.

leaves); lady's smock (*Cardamine pratensis*) (pink-lilac flowers); *Trollius*, varieties of which include *T. × cultorum* (orange-yellow flowers with abundunt foliage) and *T. europaeus* (lemon-yellow flowers with heavily dissected foliage); and finally the skunk cabbage

(*Lysichiton americanus*), with its strange yellow spathes, which is one of the most spectacular. For summer flowering, choose from giant rhubarb (*Rheum palmatum*) (creamy white or pink flower spikes and large leaves); goat's beard (*Aruncus dioicus*)

The cardinal flower (*Lobelia cardinalis*) has glorious, red-purple leaves which are trumped in late summer by the arrival of spectacular crimson-red flowers.

(creamy-white flowers); *Astilbe × arendsii* (a range of colours from deep crimson to pale pink and white flowers); bugbane (*Cimicifuga racemosa*) (tall spikes of creamy-white flowers); *Gunnera manicata* (architectural foliage); day lilies (*Hemerocallis*) (red, pink and orange flowers); hostas (blue or white flowers and large leaves); *Iris sibirica* (blue- or purple-veined flowers); *Ligularia dentata* (orange flowers and large leaves); the cardinal flower (*Lobelia cardinalis*) (scarlet flowers); and purple loosestrife (*Lythrum salicaria*) (magenta flower spikes).

Campanula cochleariifolia (syn. *C. pusilla*) is a spreading perennial with masses or tiny, bell-shaped lilac, white of pale blue flowers bursting forth in summer.

ROCK PLANTS

Before choosing from the enormous range of available alpines, plan your rock garden carefully. Many alpines are deceptively small to start with, but if you plant them close together they will be overcrowded and will not thrive. You also need to get the balance right between plants and rocks: a mass of rocks with hardly any plant cover will look uninteresting, whilst a rock garden dominated by

Tulipa aucheriana is a summer-flowering alpine. Its flowers, which rise above the grey-green leaves, are pink with yellow centres and tapered bases.

overcrowded plants will look unnatural as well as being difficult to maintain. Aim for contrast in your choice of plants, so that you have some alpines hanging down over rocks, and others growing out of crevices and gaps, and combine the more subtly coloured with those offering a bold display.

PERENNIALS

Some of the easiest alpines to grow, such as aubrieta, arabis and alyssum, will provide a splendid display of colour in spring and early summer, but for the rest of the year will hardly justify their place. Plant them with care because they are rampant growers and will simply crowd out neighbouring plants. Having said that, *Alyssum saxatile* (now more correctly called *Aurinia saxatilis*), *Arabis caucasica* and *Aubrieta deltoidea* are dependable favourites in many rock gardens. The lovely snow-in-summer (*Cerastium tomentosum*) and *Veronica filiformis* both fall into the same category and can dominate the rock garden if given the chance.

The following alpines are all reliable plants for the rock garden. Clump- or cushion-forming plants include the rock jasmine (*Androsace lanuginosa*) (lilac-pink flowers above mats of silky

Saxifraga longifolia, a hardy perennial, has long, narrow leaves that form attractive rosettes. After a few years, it will bear white flowers in late spring and summer.

leaf rosettes); thrift (*Armeria maritima*) (small flowers on leafless stalks); *Campanula cochleariifolia* (little blue bells on leafy stems) and *C. portenschlagiana* (violet-blue flowers); *Geranium dalmaticum* (deep pink flowers borne above rounded, shiny leaves); *Phlox douglasii* (mauve, purple or crimson flowers and mounds of narrow leaves); and saxifrages, including *Saxifraga burseriana*, *S. longifolia* (white) and *S. oppositifolia* (pink).

Gentiana sino-ornata, an evergreen spreading perennial, produces striking, trumpet-shaped, royal-blue flowers in autumn. It is best grown in moist soil.

Plants with more mat-like foliage include *Penstemon newberryi*, with rose-pink flowers; *Phlox subulata*, with needle-like leaves studded with white, pink, mauve or crimson flowers; and violas (pansies and violets), including *Viola cornuta* (violet to lilac or white flowers), *V. calcarata* (pansy-like flowers in lilac, purple or white) and *V. lutea* (yellow, violet, white or bicoloured flowers).

Phlox douglasii 'Rosea' is an evergreen, mound-forming perennial. In early summer, it bears a profusion of saucer-shaped, lilac-coloured flowers.

Some of the most popular and showy rock plants are gentians, and many people consider that a rock garden is not complete without these plants. Some are quite demanding to grow, and it is better to leave these until you have the skill to deal with them, but others may be planted in confidence and enjoyed in all their glory. *Gentiana septemfida* has generous heads of blue flowers from mid- to late

This *Erodium petraeum* has saucer-shaped, purple-veined flowers. A compact, mound-forming perennial it is ideal for rock gardens.

summer, whilst *G. acaulis* produces its deep blue trumpets in spring, followed by repeat flowering through the year. For those gardens with lime-free soil, the trumpet gentian (*G. sino-ornata*), with its intensely blue flowers above deep green leaves, will flower from late summer into winter. Other gentians will produce red, white and yellow flowers; ask your nursery for advice on which plants will suit your soil and will be easy to grow.

Sea thrift (*Armeria maritima*) growing in its natural habitat: on a salty cliff on the island of Coll, an island of the Inner Hebrides off the west coast of Scotland.

Another plant with blue flowers is the windflower (*Anemone blanda*). Related to it is the pasque flower (*Pulsatilla vulgaris*), which, with its finely cut leaves and solitary, bell- or cup-shaped purple flowers, is one of the loveliest in the rock garden. A third plant in this colour range is columbine (*Aquilegia flabellata*), with white-tipped, blue-mauve flowers; There is also a dwarf form, 'Nana".

Phlox subulata, a hardy perennial with needle-like leaves, will smother a rock garden with star-shaped white, pink or mauve flowers in early summer.

Some tuft-forming plants to consider are stork's bill (*Erodium petraeum*), which has dissected foliage and saucer-shaped, pink flowers; *Geranium septemfida*, whose deep blue bells are borne over large oval leaves; edelweiss (*Leontopodium alpinum*), with its narrow, grey-green leaves and ruff of furry bracts surrounding the flowers; alpine catchfly (*Lychnis alpina*), which has narrow, slightly sticky leaves and

Aurinia saxatilis (syn. *Alyssum saxatile*), an evergreen perennial, forms low clumps of grey-green leaves. In spring, it bears spikes of small, metallic-yellow flowers.

pink-purple flowers; the Welsh poppy (*Meconopsis cambrica*), whose yellow or orange flowers are borne over bright green tufts of foliage; and evening primrose (*Oenothera missouriensis*), with its striking oval, deep green leaves and large yellow flowers.

Two attractive trailing alpines are *Gentiana sino-ornata* and *Polygonum affine*, whose leathery green leaves turn bronze in autumn, and whose oblong flower-spikes are pink or rose-red.

Some tuberous-rooted perennials that you might want to consider are *Corydalis solida*, which has a single raceme of pale to deep pink or purple flowers, and some of the ever-popular cyclamens, including *C. hederifolium* with variegated foliage and pink flowers, *C. coum* with plain or variegated foliage and pale to deep pink flowers and

C. repandum (variegated leaves and magenta flowers). If you like succulents, then *Lewisia cotyledon* (large, evergreen rosettes of leaves with white to pink and purple flowers); common stonecrop (*Sedum acre*) (mats of spreading shoots covered with bright yellow flowers); and cobweb houseleek (*Sempervivum arachnoideum*) (small rosettes of cobwebbed leaves with reddish or pinkish flowers) will be sure to please. Another plant with

Campanula portenschlagiana is an evergreen perennial with small ivy-shaped leaves and a profusion of bell-shaped violet flowers in the summer.

rosettes of leaves is *Ramonda myconi*, which has flat flowers of blue, mauve or pink.

An important perennial for the rock garden is the primula. This is an enormous group containing many varied species and cultivars. The different members are suited to various soil conditions and have different requirements regarding moisture. Ask your nursery for advice.

Anemone sylvestris is a carpeting perennial that can become rampant if left unchecked. In early summer, it bears cup-shaped, white flowers.

SMALL SHRUBS

Small, slow-growing shrubs will complement the alpines in your rock garden, adding colour and variety.

Many plants in the broom family make excellent additions to the rock garden. Try *Cytisus ardoinii* 'Cottage', which has arching stems and small leaves and masses of golden pea-flowers in spring, or *Genista lydia*, which has arching stems covered in bright yellow flowers in late spring and early summer.

St John's wort (*Hypericum olympicum*) is an upright, spreading shrub with clusters of bright yellow flowers in summer, which rise above grey-green leaves.

For those who like bright flowers, *Genista lydia* fits the bill. In spring, it is absolutely swamped with a mound of bright, gold-coloured, pea-like flowers.

The daphnes are another group of attractive shrubs, including the deciduous *D. mezereum*, whose small clusters of reddish-purple or pink flowers are followed in summer by shiny red berries; for an evergreen, choose *D. petraea* 'Grandiflora', with its large pink flowers and glossy leaves. In spring, candytuft (*Iberis sempervirens*) forms mounds of leathery green foliage and has clusters of white flowers. For summer, choose from St John's wort

The rock rose (*Helianthemum*) is one of the most attractive of dwarf shrubs. Rock roses are ideal for the rock garden, spreading into large sheets, but rarely getting tall.

(*Hypericum olympicum*), with lemon-yellow flower clusters; the rock rose (*Helianthemum nummularium*), with racemes of bright yellow flowers; and *Rhododendron ferrugineum*, with pink to crimson, trumpet-shaped flowers.

DWARF CONIFERS

Not everyone appreciates dwarf conifers, and in a very small rock garden they may look out of place. They will, however, give it structure and interest in winter.

Chamaecyparis lawsoniana 'Aurea Densa' is a conifer with aromatic dark green leaves and globular cones. The male can be brick-red, while the female is green.

For deep green, rounded and compact conifers, choose from *Abies balsamea* 'Nana', a very slow-growing fir; *Picea omorika* 'Nana', a spruce, whose leaves have a white underside; *Pinus mugo* 'Humpy', a dwarf form of the mountain pine; and *P. strobus* 'Reinshaus'. If you prefer more steely blue foliage, then try *Abies concolor* 'Glauca Compacta' or *Juniperus*

communis 'Blue Pygmy'; for bright bluish foliage, try *J. squamata* 'Blue Star', one of the finest of all small conifers.

The following conifers form cones or columns: *Chamaecyparis lawsoniana* 'Ellwood's Pillar' (blue-grey columnar cypress) and *C. obtusa* 'Nana Pyramidalis' (deep green conical cypress); *Picea abies* 'Ohlendorfii' (develops from deep green dome to column) and *P. glauca* var. *albertiana* 'Conica' (bright yellow-green pyramid or cone); and *Pinus sylvestris* 'Doone Valley' (deep green cone). *Juniperus communis* 'Compressa' makes a tiny column of grey-green foliage.

Some choice golden conifers are *Chamaecyparis lawsoniana* 'Aurea Densa' (domed cypress); *Cedrus deodara* 'Golden Horizon' (semi-prostrate cedar); and *Thuja orientalis* 'Aurea Nana' (neat egg-shape with green and bronze foliage in winter).

Picea glauca var. *albertiana* 'Conica' is a narrowly conical conifer, noted for being slow-growing. It also has long leaves and smaller cones than other varieties.

INDEX

ACKNOWLEDGEMENTS

The author and publisher gratefully acknowledge the work of Robert Crawford Clarke, who has extrapolated the plans for the gardens. These plans do not necessarily reflect the original designer's plan. Where known, the garden designers are acknowledged below.

Photographs (t = top, b = bottom, l = left, r = right, m = middle)

Pat Brindley: p12t; p27t; p35b. **Jonathan Buckley**: p6. **The Garden Picture Library**: main jacket image JS Sira; jacket front flap Lamontagne; p1 Ron Sutherland; p9t Michael Paul; p11 John Glover; p12b Ron Sutherland (Paul Bangay Design); p13t Ron Sutherland (Chelsea Flower Show, London, Hiroshi Nanamori Design); p13b Jerry Pavia; p17t Alan Bedding; p17bl Howard Rice; p18 JS Sira; p19t Ron Sutherland (Michelle Osborne Design); p19b Ron Sutherland (Smyth Garden, Jersey, Anthony Paul Design); p23t Marianne Majerus (John Brooks Design, BBC Garden); p25 Ron Sutherland (Anthony Paul Design); p34 Ron Sutherland (Anthony Paul Design); p35t John Glover; p49 Brian Carter; p51 Jerry Pavia; p54 JS Sira (design by Japanese Garden Company, Chelsea Flower Show, London 1991); p55l Ron Sutherland (Anthony Paul Design); p56 Ron Sutherland (Paul Flinton Design, Australia); p57t Lamontagne p57b Alan Mitchell; p58 Ron Sutherland (Anthony Paul Design); p59t Ron Sutherland; p59b Ron Sutherland (Anthony Paul Design); p67t Ron Sutherland; p69 Ron Sutherland (Paul Flemming Design, Australia); p71 Ron Sutherland (Hiroshi Nanamori Design); p73 Ron Sutherland (Anthony Paul Design); p90tl Brian Carter; p90bl JS Sira; p90tr John Glover; p90br John Glover; p91l Sunniva Harte; p91t Steven Wooster; p91b Dennis Davis; p92t John Glover; p92m John Glover; p92tr Howard Rice; p92br Howard Rice. **Peter McHoy**: p14; p14b (design by Alpine Garden Society); p15; p21 (design by Kathleen McHoy); p21b; p31; p36; p37; p38; p39; p40; p41; p42; p43; p45 (design by Jean Bishop); p53 (design by Natural and Oriental Water Gardens)p60; p61; p62; p63; p64; p65; p75.